50 Japanese Mastery Recipes for Home

By: Kelly Johnson

Table of Contents

- Sushi rolls
- Miso soup
- Tempura
- Ramen noodles
- Teriyaki chicken
- Sashimi
- Gyoza (dumplings)
- Udon noodles
- Yakitori (grilled chicken skewers)
- Chawanmushi (savory egg custard)
- Tonkatsu (breaded and fried pork cutlet)
- Okonomiyaki (Japanese savory pancake)
- Onigiri (rice balls)
- Takoyaki (octopus balls)
- Katsu curry (breaded and fried meat with curry sauce)
- Nikujaga (Japanese beef stew)
- Shabu-shabu (Japanese hot pot)
- Oden (Japanese stew with fish cakes and vegetables)
- Chirashi sushi (scattered sushi)
- Oyakodon (chicken and egg rice bowl)
- Nabemono (Japanese one-pot dishes)
- Yakiniku (Japanese grilled meat)
- Omurice (Japanese omelette rice)
- Hiyashi chuka (cold ramen salad)
- Soba noodles
- Karaage (Japanese fried chicken)
- Ankake yakisoba (stir-fried noodles with thick sauce)
- Hambagu (Japanese hamburger steak)
- Tonjiru (pork miso soup)
- Tamagoyaki (Japanese rolled omelette)
- Dorayaki (Japanese pancakes filled with sweet red bean paste)
- Yakisoba (Japanese stir-fried noodles)
- Ochazuke (rice with tea poured over)
- Chazuke (Japanese rice soup)
- Oshizushi (pressed sushi)

- Tofu dishes (such as agedashi tofu or tofu steak)
- Kaiseki (traditional Japanese multi-course meal)
- Matcha desserts (such as matcha ice cream or matcha cake)
- Sake-steamed clams
- Horenso no goma-ae (spinach with sesame dressing)
- Sunomono (Japanese cucumber salad)
- Zaru soba (cold buckwheat noodles with dipping sauce)
- Gomoku gohan (rice cooked with mixed vegetables)
- Anmitsu (Japanese dessert with agar jelly and fruits)
- Katsudon (breaded and fried pork cutlet rice bowl)
- Mochi (Japanese rice cakes)
- Oshiruko (sweet red bean soup)
- Yudofu (hot tofu)
- Gyunabe (beef hot pot)
- Hamachi kama (grilled yellowtail collar)

Sushi rolls

California Roll Recipe:

Ingredients:

- 2 cups sushi rice
- 2 1/2 cups water
- 1/2 cup rice vinegar
- 2 tablespoons sugar
- 1 teaspoon salt
- 4 sheets nori (seaweed)
- 1 ripe avocado, sliced
- 1/2 cucumber, julienned
- 8 imitation crab sticks (or real crab if preferred)
- Soy sauce, for serving
- Wasabi, for serving
- Pickled ginger, for serving

Instructions:

1. Rinse the sushi rice under cold water until the water runs clear. Combine the rinsed rice and water in a rice cooker and cook according to the manufacturer's instructions.
2. In a small saucepan, combine the rice vinegar, sugar, and salt. Heat over low heat, stirring until the sugar and salt are dissolved. Remove from heat and let the mixture cool.
3. Once the rice is cooked, transfer it to a large bowl and gently fold in the vinegar mixture. Be careful not to smash the rice grains. Let the rice cool to room temperature.
4. Place a sheet of nori on a bamboo sushi mat or a clean kitchen towel. With wet hands, spread about 1/2 cup of sushi rice evenly over the nori, leaving a 1-inch border at the top edge.
5. Arrange slices of avocado, cucumber, and crab sticks horizontally across the rice-covered nori sheet.
6. Starting from the bottom edge, tightly roll the sushi using the bamboo mat or kitchen towel, pressing gently as you roll to shape the roll.

7. Repeat the process with the remaining nori sheets and fillings.
8. Using a sharp knife dipped in water, slice each roll into 6-8 pieces.
9. Serve the sushi rolls with soy sauce, wasabi, and pickled ginger on the side.

Enjoy your homemade California rolls! Adjust the fillings according to your preferences, and feel free to experiment with different ingredients to create your own unique sushi rolls.

Miso soup

Ingredients:

- 4 cups dashi (Japanese fish and/or seaweed stock) or vegetable broth
- 3 tablespoons miso paste (white or red)
- 2 green onions, thinly sliced
- 1/2 block (about 4 ounces) firm tofu, diced
- 1 tablespoon wakame seaweed, soaked in water and drained (optional)
- 1 teaspoon soy sauce (optional)
- 1 teaspoon mirin (Japanese sweet rice wine) (optional)
- 1 teaspoon sesame oil (optional)
- Toppings: sliced green onions, tofu cubes, wakame seaweed, sliced mushrooms, cooked shrimp, or any other desired toppings

Instructions:

1. In a pot, bring the dashi or vegetable broth to a gentle simmer over medium heat.
2. In a small bowl, dilute the miso paste with a small amount of hot broth from the pot until smooth.
3. Add the diluted miso paste to the pot of simmering broth, stirring well to incorporate.
4. Add the sliced green onions, diced tofu, and soaked wakame seaweed (if using) to the pot.
5. If desired, add soy sauce, mirin, and sesame oil for additional flavor.
6. Allow the soup to simmer for a few minutes until heated through and the flavors have melded together. Be careful not to boil the miso soup, as boiling can reduce its flavor.
7. Taste the miso soup and adjust the seasoning if needed. Add more miso paste for a stronger flavor, or more hot broth to dilute the taste.
8. Ladle the miso soup into bowls and garnish with additional toppings such as sliced green onions, tofu cubes, or wakame seaweed.
9. Serve the miso soup hot as a comforting and nourishing appetizer or main dish.

Enjoy the comforting warmth and savory flavor of homemade miso soup! Feel free to customize the soup with your favorite toppings and adjust the seasoning to suit your taste preferences.

Tempura

Ingredients:

- Assorted vegetables (such as bell peppers, sweet potatoes, onions, zucchini, mushrooms, or green beans), sliced into bite-sized pieces
- Seafood (such as shrimp, squid, or fish fillets), cleaned and deveined (optional)
- 1 cup all-purpose flour
- 1/2 cup cornstarch
- 1 teaspoon baking powder
- 1 egg, beaten
- 1 cup ice-cold water
- Vegetable oil, for frying
- Salt, to taste
- Tempura dipping sauce (tentsuyu), for serving (recipe below)

Instructions:

1. Prepare the vegetables and seafood by slicing them into bite-sized pieces. Pat them dry with paper towels to remove excess moisture, which helps the batter adhere better.
2. In a large mixing bowl, combine the all-purpose flour, cornstarch, and baking powder.
3. In a separate bowl, beat the egg and then add ice-cold water. Gradually pour the egg mixture into the dry ingredients, whisking until just combined. It's okay if the batter is slightly lumpy.
4. Heat vegetable oil in a deep frying pan or pot to 350°F (180°C). You can test if the oil is ready by dropping a small amount of batter into the oil – it should sizzle and float to the surface.
5. Dip the prepared vegetables and seafood into the batter, coating them evenly. Shake off any excess batter before gently placing them into the hot oil.
6. Fry the tempura in batches, making sure not to overcrowd the pan. Fry until golden brown and crispy, about 2-3 minutes for vegetables and 3-4 minutes for seafood. Use a slotted spoon or tongs to remove the tempura from the oil and drain them on paper towels.
7. Sprinkle the hot tempura with a pinch of salt as soon as they come out of the oil.

8. Serve the tempura immediately with tempura dipping sauce (tentsuyu) on the side.

Tempura Dipping Sauce (Tentsuyu):

Ingredients:

- 1/2 cup dashi (Japanese fish and/or seaweed stock)
- 2 tablespoons soy sauce
- 2 tablespoons mirin (Japanese sweet rice wine)
- 1 teaspoon sugar

Instructions:

1. In a small saucepan, combine the dashi, soy sauce, mirin, and sugar. Bring to a simmer over medium heat, stirring until the sugar is dissolved.
2. Remove the saucepan from the heat and let the tempura dipping sauce cool to room temperature.
3. Serve the tempura dipping sauce alongside the hot tempura for dipping.

Enjoy your crispy and delicious homemade tempura with your favorite dipping sauce!

Ramen noodles

Ingredients:

- 2 cups all-purpose flour
- 1 teaspoon salt
- 2 large eggs
- 1 tablespoon water (optional, if needed)

Instructions:

1. In a large mixing bowl, combine the all-purpose flour and salt. Make a well in the center of the flour mixture.
2. Crack the eggs into the well. Using a fork or your fingers, gradually mix the eggs into the flour mixture until a dough starts to form.
3. Once the dough begins to come together, knead it with your hands until it becomes smooth and elastic, about 5-10 minutes. If the dough is too dry, you can add a tablespoon of water at a time until it reaches the right consistency.
4. Once the dough is smooth and elastic, shape it into a ball and wrap it tightly in plastic wrap. Let the dough rest at room temperature for at least 30 minutes, or up to 2 hours. This allows the gluten to relax and makes the dough easier to roll out.
5. After the resting period, unwrap the dough and divide it into 4 equal portions.
6. On a lightly floured surface, roll out each portion of dough into a thin sheet, about 1/16 to 1/8 inch thick. You can use a rolling pin or pasta machine to help you achieve the desired thickness.
7. Once rolled out, dust the sheets of dough with a little more flour to prevent sticking. Then, use a sharp knife or pasta cutter to cut the dough into thin strips, about 1/8 to 1/4 inch wide, to make your ramen noodles.
8. Once all the noodles are cut, you can cook them immediately in boiling water for about 2-3 minutes until they are tender but still slightly firm (al dente). Alternatively, you can let the noodles air dry for a few hours or overnight before cooking them.
9. After cooking, drain the noodles and rinse them under cold water to stop the cooking process and remove excess starch. Then, use the noodles immediately in your favorite ramen soup or dish.

Enjoy your homemade ramen noodles in a delicious bowl of homemade ramen soup or stir-fry! Adjust the thickness and width of the noodles to your liking, and feel free to experiment with different flavors and ingredients to create your own unique ramen dishes.

Teriyaki chicken

Ingredients:

- 4 boneless, skinless chicken breasts
- 1/2 cup soy sauce
- 1/4 cup mirin (Japanese sweet rice wine)
- 2 tablespoons honey or brown sugar
- 2 cloves garlic, minced
- 1 teaspoon grated ginger
- 1 tablespoon cornstarch
- 2 tablespoons water
- 1 tablespoon vegetable oil
- Optional garnish: sliced green onions and sesame seeds

Instructions:

1. In a bowl, whisk together the soy sauce, mirin, honey or brown sugar, minced garlic, and grated ginger to make the teriyaki sauce.
2. Place the chicken breasts in a shallow dish or resealable plastic bag. Pour half of the teriyaki sauce over the chicken, reserving the other half for later. Marinate the chicken in the refrigerator for at least 30 minutes, or up to 2 hours, turning occasionally to ensure even coating.
3. In a small bowl, mix the cornstarch and water to make a slurry.
4. Heat the vegetable oil in a large skillet or frying pan over medium-high heat. Once hot, add the marinated chicken breasts to the pan, discarding any excess marinade. Cook the chicken for 5-6 minutes on each side, or until browned and cooked through, with no pink in the center. The internal temperature of the chicken should reach 165°F (75°C).
5. While the chicken is cooking, transfer the reserved teriyaki sauce to a small saucepan. Bring the sauce to a simmer over medium heat.
6. Stir the cornstarch slurry into the simmering teriyaki sauce. Cook, stirring constantly, until the sauce thickens and becomes glossy, about 1-2 minutes.
7. Once the chicken is cooked through, remove it from the pan and let it rest for a few minutes before slicing it thinly.
8. Drizzle the thickened teriyaki sauce over the sliced chicken. Garnish with sliced green onions and sesame seeds, if desired.

9. Serve the teriyaki chicken hot with steamed rice and your favorite vegetables for a delicious and satisfying meal.

Enjoy your homemade teriyaki chicken with its sweet and savory flavors! Adjust the sweetness and thickness of the sauce to your liking, and feel free to add extra garlic or ginger for more flavor.

Sashimi

Ingredients:

- 8 ounces of sushi-grade fish or seafood (such as tuna, salmon, yellowtail, or scallops)
- Soy sauce (shoyu), for dipping
- Wasabi paste, optional, for mixing with soy sauce
- Pickled ginger (gari), for serving
- Shiso leaves or thinly sliced cucumber, for garnish (optional)

Instructions:

1. Start by selecting fresh, sushi-grade fish or seafood from a reputable fishmonger or specialty grocery store. Make sure the fish is suitable for raw consumption and has been properly handled and stored.
2. Rinse the fish under cold water and pat it dry with paper towels. Use a sharp knife to carefully remove any skin and bones, if necessary. Slice the fish into thin, even pieces, cutting against the grain for optimal texture.
3. Arrange the sliced fish on a serving platter in an attractive manner. You can create a decorative layout by overlapping the slices or arranging them in a circular pattern.
4. Optional: If you're using wasabi paste, mix a small amount into the soy sauce to create a dipping sauce with extra flavor and heat.
5. Serve the sashimi immediately with soy sauce for dipping and pickled ginger on the side to cleanse the palate between bites. You can also garnish the platter with shiso leaves or thinly sliced cucumber for added freshness and presentation.
6. Enjoy the homemade sashimi as a delicious appetizer or part of a traditional Japanese meal. Savor the delicate flavors and textures of the fresh fish or seafood, dipping each piece lightly into the soy sauce mixture before eating.
7. Remember to handle raw fish with care and follow proper food safety guidelines to minimize the risk of foodborne illness. It's best to consume sashimi shortly after preparing it to ensure the freshest taste and quality.

Homemade sashimi is a delightful way to experience the purity and simplicity of raw fish or seafood. Experiment with different types of fish and seafood to discover your favorite combinations, and enjoy the elegant flavors of this traditional Japanese delicacy.

Gyoza (dumplings)

Ingredients:

- 1/2 pound ground pork
- 2 cups cabbage, finely shredded
- 2 green onions, finely chopped
- 2 cloves garlic, minced
- 1 tablespoon ginger, minced
- 2 tablespoons soy sauce
- 1 tablespoon sesame oil
- 1 teaspoon sugar
- 1/2 teaspoon salt
- 1/4 teaspoon black pepper
- 30-40 gyoza wrappers
- 2 tablespoons vegetable oil
- 1/2 cup water

Instructions:

1. In a large mixing bowl, combine the ground pork, shredded cabbage, chopped green onions, minced garlic, minced ginger, soy sauce, sesame oil, sugar, salt, and black pepper. Mix well until all the ingredients are evenly incorporated.
2. Place a small spoonful of the filling mixture (about 1 teaspoon) in the center of a gyoza wrapper. Dip your finger in water and moisten the edges of the wrapper. Fold the wrapper in half to form a half-moon shape, then crimp the edges to seal the dumpling. Repeat with the remaining filling and wrappers.
3. Heat 1 tablespoon of vegetable oil in a large non-stick skillet over medium-high heat. Once hot, arrange the gyoza in the skillet in a single layer, making sure they are not touching each other. Cook for 2-3 minutes, or until the bottoms are golden brown.
4. Carefully pour 1/2 cup of water into the skillet, then immediately cover it with a lid. Reduce the heat to medium-low and let the gyoza steam for 6-8 minutes, or until the wrappers are translucent and the filling is cooked through.
5. Remove the lid and let any remaining water evaporate. Drizzle the remaining tablespoon of vegetable oil around the edges of the skillet and cook the gyoza uncovered for an additional 1-2 minutes, or until the bottoms are crispy.

6. Use a spatula to transfer the cooked gyoza to a serving plate. Serve them hot with dipping sauce made from soy sauce, rice vinegar, and a splash of sesame oil.

Enjoy your homemade gyoza as a delicious appetizer or part of a Japanese-inspired meal! Adjust the filling ingredients to your taste preferences, and experiment with different dipping sauces for added flavor.

Udon noodles

Ingredients:

- 2 cups all-purpose flour
- 3/4 cup water
- 1 teaspoon salt
- Additional flour for dusting

Instructions:

1. In a large mixing bowl, combine the all-purpose flour and salt. Make a well in the center of the flour mixture.
2. Gradually add the water to the well while stirring with a fork or chopsticks. Continue mixing until a rough dough forms.
3. Turn the dough out onto a clean, floured surface. Knead the dough for about 5-10 minutes, or until it becomes smooth and elastic. If the dough is too sticky, you can add a little more flour as needed.
4. Once the dough is kneaded, shape it into a ball and wrap it tightly in plastic wrap. Let the dough rest at room temperature for at least 30 minutes, or up to 2 hours. This allows the gluten to relax and makes the dough easier to roll out.
5. After the resting period, unwrap the dough and divide it into 4 equal portions.
6. On a clean, floured surface, roll out each portion of dough into a thin rectangle, about 1/8 inch thick. You can use a rolling pin to help you achieve the desired thickness.
7. Once rolled out, fold the dough in half lengthwise, then fold it in half again widthwise. Use a sharp knife to cut the folded dough into thin strips, about 1/4 inch wide, to make your udon noodles.
8. Unfold the cut noodles and dust them lightly with flour to prevent sticking.
9. Bring a large pot of water to a boil over high heat. Add the udon noodles to the boiling water and cook them for about 8-10 minutes, or until they are tender but still slightly firm (al dente). Stir occasionally to prevent sticking.
10. Once cooked, drain the udon noodles in a colander and rinse them under cold water to stop the cooking process and remove excess starch.
11. Serve the udon noodles hot in your favorite soup or broth, or toss them with a stir-fry sauce and your choice of vegetables and protein for a delicious noodle dish.

Enjoy your homemade udon noodles as a comforting and satisfying meal! Experiment with different toppings and sauces to create your own unique udon creations.

Yakitori (grilled chicken skewers)

Ingredients:

- 1 lb boneless, skinless chicken thighs or breast, cut into bite-sized pieces
- 1/4 cup soy sauce
- 1/4 cup mirin (Japanese sweet rice wine)
- 2 tablespoons sake (Japanese rice wine) or dry white wine
- 2 tablespoons granulated sugar
- 2 cloves garlic, minced
- 1 teaspoon grated ginger
- Bamboo skewers, soaked in water for at least 30 minutes

Instructions:

1. In a bowl, combine the soy sauce, mirin, sake, sugar, minced garlic, and grated ginger to make the yakitori marinade.
2. Add the chicken pieces to the marinade and toss to coat evenly. Cover the bowl and refrigerate the chicken for at least 1 hour, or up to overnight, to allow the flavors to meld together.
3. Preheat your grill or broiler to medium-high heat. If using a grill, lightly oil the grates to prevent sticking.
4. While the grill is heating, thread the marinated chicken pieces onto the soaked bamboo skewers, leaving a little space between each piece.
5. Once the grill is hot, place the chicken skewers on the grill or under the broiler. Cook for about 4-5 minutes on each side, or until the chicken is cooked through and nicely charred on the outside. Brush the skewers with any remaining marinade while cooking for extra flavor.
6. Once the chicken is cooked through, remove the skewers from the grill or broiler and transfer them to a serving platter.
7. Serve the yakitori hot as an appetizer or main dish, garnished with chopped green onions or sesame seeds if desired. Enjoy!

Yakitori is delicious on its own or served with steamed rice and a side of vegetables for a complete meal. Feel free to customize the marinade with your favorite seasonings or add vegetables and other ingredients to the skewers for variety.

Chawanmushi (savory egg custard)

Ingredients:

- 2 cups dashi (Japanese fish and/or seaweed stock)
- 4 large eggs
- 1 tablespoon soy sauce
- 1 tablespoon mirin (Japanese sweet rice wine)
- 1/2 teaspoon salt
- 1 teaspoon sesame oil
- 1/4 cup cooked shrimp, chopped (optional)
- 1/4 cup cooked chicken, shredded (optional)
- 2 fresh shiitake mushrooms, thinly sliced (optional)
- 2 small pieces kamaboko (Japanese fish cake), thinly sliced (optional)
- 2 sprigs mitsuba (Japanese parsley) or chopped green onions, for garnish

Instructions:

1. In a mixing bowl, whisk together the dashi, eggs, soy sauce, mirin, salt, and sesame oil until well combined. Strain the mixture through a fine-mesh sieve to remove any lumps.
2. Prepare your chawanmushi cups or ramekins by lightly greasing them with a little sesame oil or cooking spray.
3. Divide the optional ingredients (shrimp, chicken, mushrooms, kamaboko) evenly among the cups or ramekins.
4. Carefully pour the egg mixture into the prepared cups or ramekins, filling them almost to the top.
5. Cover each cup or ramekin tightly with plastic wrap to prevent water from getting into the custard during steaming.
6. Place the cups or ramekins in a steamer basket or on a steaming rack, making sure they are not touching each other.
7. Fill a large pot or wok with water and bring it to a simmer over medium heat. Once the water is simmering, carefully place the steamer basket or rack over the pot, making sure the cups or ramekins are securely positioned.
8. Steam the chawanmushi for about 15-20 minutes, or until the custard is set but still slightly jiggly in the center. To check for doneness, insert a toothpick into the center of the custard—if it comes out clean, the custard is ready.

9. Once cooked, carefully remove the cups or ramekins from the steamer and let them cool slightly before serving.
10. Garnish the chawanmushi with fresh mitsuba or chopped green onions before serving.

Enjoy your homemade chawanmushi as a delicate and flavorful appetizer or side dish! Experiment with different ingredients and variations to create your own unique version of this traditional Japanese dish.

Tonkatsu (breaded and fried pork cutlet)

Ingredients:

- 4 pork loin or pork tenderloin cutlets, about 1/2 inch thick
- Salt and pepper, to taste
- All-purpose flour, for dredging
- 2 large eggs, beaten
- 1 cup panko breadcrumbs
- Vegetable oil, for frying
- Tonkatsu sauce, for serving (can be found in Asian grocery stores or made at home using Worcestershire sauce, ketchup, soy sauce, and sugar)

Instructions:

1. Start by preparing the pork cutlets. Use a meat mallet to gently pound the cutlets to an even thickness of about 1/4 inch. Season both sides of the cutlets with salt and pepper.
2. Set up a breading station with three shallow dishes. Place the flour in the first dish, beaten eggs in the second dish, and panko breadcrumbs in the third dish.
3. Dredge each pork cutlet in the flour, shaking off any excess. Dip the floured cutlets into the beaten eggs, ensuring they are evenly coated. Finally, coat the cutlets in the panko breadcrumbs, pressing gently to adhere.
4. Heat vegetable oil in a large skillet or frying pan over medium-high heat. The oil should be hot enough to sizzle when a breadcrumb is added, but not smoking.
5. Carefully add the breaded pork cutlets to the hot oil, working in batches if necessary to avoid overcrowding the pan. Fry the cutlets for 3-4 minutes on each side, or until golden brown and cooked through. The internal temperature of the pork should reach 145°F (63°C).
6. Once cooked, transfer the tonkatsu to a wire rack or paper towels to drain and rest for a few minutes.
7. Slice the tonkatsu into strips or serve it whole, accompanied by tonkatsu sauce for dipping.
8. Serve the tonkatsu hot with steamed rice, shredded cabbage, and a drizzle of tonkatsu sauce.

Enjoy your homemade tonkatsu as a comforting and satisfying Japanese meal! Adjust the seasoning and cooking time to your taste preferences, and feel free to experiment with different cuts of pork or variations of the dish.

Okonomiyaki (Japanese savory pancake)

Ingredients:

- 2 cups cabbage, finely shredded
- 1 cup all-purpose flour
- 2/3 cup dashi (Japanese fish and/or seaweed stock) or water
- 2 large eggs
- 1/4 cup green onions, finely chopped
- 1/4 cup tenkasu (tempura scraps) or panko breadcrumbs
- 1/4 cup cooked shrimp, chopped (optional)
- 1/4 cup cooked squid, chopped (optional)
- 1/4 cup thinly sliced pork belly or bacon (optional)
- Vegetable oil, for frying
- Okonomiyaki sauce (can be found in Asian grocery stores)
- Japanese mayonnaise
- Aonori (dried green seaweed flakes), for garnish (optional)
- Katsuobushi (bonito flakes), for garnish (optional)

Instructions:

1. In a large mixing bowl, combine the shredded cabbage, all-purpose flour, dashi or water, eggs, green onions, and tenkasu or panko breadcrumbs. Mix until well combined and the batter has a thick consistency.
2. If using optional ingredients such as shrimp, squid, or pork belly, fold them into the batter until evenly distributed.
3. Heat a non-stick skillet or griddle over medium heat and lightly oil the surface.
4. Pour a portion of the batter onto the skillet to form a pancake, using a spatula to shape it into a round disc about 1/2 inch thick.
5. Arrange thinly sliced pork belly or bacon on top of the pancake if desired.
6. Cook the okonomiyaki for about 4-5 minutes on each side, or until golden brown and cooked through. Use a spatula to carefully flip the pancake halfway through cooking.
7. Once cooked, transfer the okonomiyaki to a serving plate.
8. Drizzle okonomiyaki sauce and Japanese mayonnaise over the top of the pancake in a crisscross pattern.
9. Sprinkle aonori (dried seaweed flakes) and katsuobushi (bonito flakes) over the sauce and mayonnaise.

10. Serve the okonomiyaki hot, cut into wedges, and enjoy!

Feel free to customize your okonomiyaki with additional toppings such as sliced mushrooms, cheese, or even kimchi for extra flavor. Adjust the thickness of the pancake and cooking time based on your preferences. Okonomiyaki is a versatile dish that can be enjoyed as a snack, appetizer, or main course.

Onigiri (rice balls)

Ingredients:

- 2 cups sushi rice
- 2 1/2 cups water
- 1/4 cup rice vinegar
- 2 tablespoons sugar
- 1 teaspoon salt
- Fillings of your choice (such as grilled salmon, tuna mayo, pickled plum, cooked chicken, or vegetables)
- Nori seaweed sheets, cut into strips (optional)
- Salt, for seasoning hands (optional)
- Onigiri molds (optional)

Instructions:

1. Rinse the sushi rice under cold water until the water runs clear. Combine the rinsed rice and water in a rice cooker and cook according to the manufacturer's instructions. Alternatively, you can cook the rice on the stovetop.
2. In a small saucepan, combine the rice vinegar, sugar, and salt. Heat over low heat, stirring until the sugar and salt are dissolved. Remove from heat and let the mixture cool.
3. Once the rice is cooked, transfer it to a large bowl and gently fold in the vinegar mixture. Be careful not to smash the rice grains. Let the rice cool to room temperature.
4. Prepare your fillings of choice. You can use leftover cooked proteins such as salmon, tuna, chicken, or vegetables, or make fillings specifically for onigiri.
5. To shape the onigiri, wet your hands with water or sprinkle them with a little salt to prevent the rice from sticking. Take a small handful of rice and flatten it in the palm of your hand.
6. Place a spoonful of filling in the center of the rice and gently fold the rice around the filling to enclose it completely. Use your hands to shape the rice into a triangle, ball, or cylindrical shape.
7. If using nori seaweed strips, wrap them around the outside of the onigiri to help hold its shape and add flavor.

8. Repeat the process with the remaining rice and fillings until you have made all of the onigiri.
9. Serve the onigiri immediately, or wrap them individually in plastic wrap to keep them fresh for later. Onigiri is best enjoyed at room temperature.

Onigiri is a versatile snack that can be customized with your favorite fillings and flavors.

Get creative and experiment with different combinations to find your perfect rice ball!

Takoyaki (octopus balls)

Ingredients:

- 1 1/4 cups all-purpose flour
- 2 cups dashi (Japanese fish and/or seaweed stock)
- 2 large eggs
- 1/2 teaspoon salt
- 1/4 teaspoon baking powder
- 1/2 cup finely chopped cooked octopus (about 1 small octopus)
- 1/4 cup chopped green onions
- 1/4 cup tenkasu (tempura scraps)
- 1/4 cup pickled ginger, chopped
- Takoyaki sauce (can be found in Asian grocery stores or made at home using Worcestershire sauce, ketchup, soy sauce, and sugar)
- Japanese mayonnaise
- Aonori (dried green seaweed flakes)
- Katsuobushi (bonito flakes)

Instructions:

1. In a large mixing bowl, whisk together the all-purpose flour, dashi, eggs, salt, and baking powder until smooth. Let the batter rest for 15-30 minutes.
2. Heat a takoyaki pan over medium heat and lightly grease the molds with vegetable oil or cooking spray.
3. Once the pan is hot, pour the batter into each mold until it's about three-quarters full.
4. Add a small amount of chopped octopus, green onions, tenkasu, and pickled ginger to each mold.
5. Let the takoyaki cook for a few minutes until the edges start to set and become golden brown. Use a skewer or chopsticks to flip each takoyaki ball over so that the uncooked batter can cook evenly.
6. Continue cooking and turning the takoyaki balls until they are evenly browned and cooked through, about 8-10 minutes in total.
7. Once the takoyaki are cooked, transfer them to a serving plate and drizzle with takoyaki sauce and Japanese mayonnaise.
8. Sprinkle aonori and katsuobushi over the top of the takoyaki for extra flavor and garnish.

9. Serve the takoyaki hot and enjoy immediately!

Takoyaki is best enjoyed fresh off the grill, so serve them as soon as they're cooked for the crispiest texture. Be careful when handling the hot takoyaki pan and flipping the balls to ensure they cook evenly. Experiment with different fillings and toppings to create your own unique takoyaki variations!

Katsu curry (breaded and fried meat with curry sauce)

Ingredients:

For the chicken katsu:

- 2 boneless, skinless chicken breasts
- Salt and pepper to taste
- 1/2 cup all-purpose flour
- 2 eggs, beaten
- 1 cup panko breadcrumbs
- Vegetable oil for frying

For the curry sauce:

- 1 tablespoon vegetable oil
- 1 onion, finely chopped
- 2 carrots, diced
- 2 potatoes, diced
- 2 cloves garlic, minced
- 2 tablespoons curry powder
- 1 tablespoon garam masala
- 1 tablespoon flour
- 2 cups chicken or vegetable broth
- 2 tablespoons soy sauce
- 1 tablespoon honey or sugar
- Salt and pepper to taste

For serving:

- Cooked rice
- Shredded cabbage or pickles (optional)

Instructions:

1. Start by preparing the chicken breasts. Place them between two sheets of plastic wrap and pound them to an even thickness, about 1/2 inch thick. Season both sides with salt and pepper.
2. Set up a breading station. Place the flour, beaten eggs, and panko breadcrumbs each in separate shallow bowls.
3. Dredge the chicken breasts in the flour, shaking off any excess. Dip them into the beaten eggs, then coat them with the panko breadcrumbs, pressing gently to adhere.
4. Heat vegetable oil in a large skillet over medium-high heat. Fry the breaded chicken breasts until golden brown and cooked through, about 4-5 minutes per side. Transfer to a paper towel-lined plate to drain excess oil.
5. While the chicken is frying, prepare the curry sauce. Heat 1 tablespoon of vegetable oil in a separate pot over medium heat. Add the chopped onion and cook until softened, about 5 minutes.
6. Add the diced carrots, potatoes, and minced garlic to the pot. Cook for another 5 minutes, stirring occasionally.
7. Sprinkle the curry powder, garam masala, and flour over the vegetables. Stir well to coat.
8. Gradually pour in the chicken or vegetable broth, stirring constantly to prevent lumps from forming. Bring the mixture to a simmer and cook until the vegetables are tender and the sauce has thickened, about 15-20 minutes.
9. Stir in the soy sauce and honey or sugar. Season with salt and pepper to taste.
10. To serve, slice the chicken katsu into strips and place on top of cooked rice. Ladle the curry sauce over the chicken and rice. Serve with shredded cabbage or pickles on the side, if desired.

Enjoy your homemade chicken katsu curry!

Nikujaga (Japanese beef stew)

Ingredients:

- 400g thinly sliced beef (such as beef chuck or ribeye)
- 2 large potatoes, peeled and cut into chunks
- 1 onion, thinly sliced
- 1 carrot, peeled and sliced
- 2 tablespoons vegetable oil
- 3 cups dashi (Japanese soup stock)
- 1/4 cup soy sauce
- 2 tablespoons mirin (Japanese sweet rice wine)
- 2 tablespoons sugar
- 2 green onions, sliced (for garnish)
- Optional: 1 tablespoon sake (Japanese rice wine)

Instructions:

1. Heat vegetable oil in a large pot or deep skillet over medium heat. Add the thinly sliced beef and cook until browned.
2. Add the sliced onion and cook until softened and translucent.
3. Pour in the dashi (Japanese soup stock) and bring to a simmer.
4. Add the soy sauce, mirin, sugar, and sake (if using) to the pot. Stir well to combine.
5. Add the potato chunks and carrot slices to the pot. Cover and simmer for about 15-20 minutes, or until the vegetables are tender and the flavors have melded together.
6. Once the vegetables are cooked through, taste the broth and adjust seasoning if necessary, adding more soy sauce or sugar according to your preference.
7. Serve the Nikujaga hot, garnished with sliced green onions. Enjoy with steamed rice on the side.

Nikujaga is a versatile dish, so feel free to customize it to your liking by adding other vegetables such as mushrooms or green beans. It's a hearty and comforting meal that's perfect for colder days!

Shabu-shabu (Japanese hot pot)

Ingredients:

For the broth:

- 6 cups dashi (Japanese soup stock)
- 1/4 cup soy sauce
- 2 tablespoons mirin (Japanese sweet rice wine)
- 2 tablespoons sake (Japanese rice wine)
- 2 cloves garlic, crushed (optional)
- 1-inch piece of ginger, thinly sliced (optional)

For the hot pot:

- 400g thinly sliced beef (sirloin or ribeye)
- Assorted vegetables such as napa cabbage, bok choy, mushrooms, carrots, and green onions, thinly sliced or cut into bite-sized pieces
- Tofu, sliced
- Udon noodles (optional)
- Dipping sauces: ponzu sauce, sesame sauce, or goma dare (sesame sauce)

Instructions:

1. Prepare the broth by combining dashi, soy sauce, mirin, sake, garlic, and ginger in a large pot. Bring to a boil, then reduce heat and let it simmer for about 10 minutes to allow the flavors to meld together. You can adjust the seasoning according to your taste.
2. Arrange the thinly sliced beef, assorted vegetables, tofu, and udon noodles on a large platter or in individual plates.
3. Set up a portable gas or electric hot pot on the dining table. If you don't have a portable hot pot, you can use a regular pot on a portable burner.
4. Once the broth is simmering, each diner can take turns placing slices of meat into the broth using chopsticks or a small wire ladle. Swish the meat back and forth in the broth for a few seconds until it's cooked to your desired doneness. This usually takes only about 10-15 seconds.

5. Remove the cooked meat from the broth and dip it into your favorite dipping sauce before eating.
6. After enjoying the meat, you can add the assorted vegetables, tofu, and udon noodles to the hot pot and cook them until tender.
7. Serve the cooked ingredients with steamed rice and additional dipping sauces on the side.

Shabu-shabu is a fun and interactive meal to enjoy with family and friends. It's perfect for gatherings and special occasions, and you can customize it with your favorite ingredients and dipping sauces. Enjoy!

Oden (Japanese stew with fish cakes and vegetables)

Ingredients:

- 6 cups dashi (Japanese soup stock)
- 1/4 cup soy sauce
- 2 tablespoons mirin (Japanese sweet rice wine)
- 1 tablespoon sugar
- 1 tablespoon sake (Japanese rice wine)
- 1 piece kombu (dried kelp), about 4 inches long
- Assorted Oden ingredients such as:
    - Fish cakes (chikuwa, kamaboko, hanpen)
    - Tofu (firm or silken)
    - Daikon radish, peeled and cut into thick rounds
    - Konnyaku (konjac), sliced into thick rounds
    - Hard-boiled eggs, peeled
    - Japanese mustard (karashi) for serving (optional)

Instructions:

1. In a large pot, combine dashi, soy sauce, mirin, sugar, sake, and kombu. Bring to a boil over medium-high heat, then reduce heat to low and simmer for about 10 minutes to allow the flavors to meld together.
2. While the broth is simmering, prepare the Oden ingredients. Cut the fish cakes into bite-sized pieces, slice the tofu into squares or rectangles, cut the daikon radish into thick rounds, slice the konnyaku into thick rounds, and peel the hard-boiled eggs.
3. Once the broth is ready, add the daikon radish and konnyaku slices to the pot. Simmer for about 10-15 minutes, or until the daikon radish is tender.
4. Add the fish cakes, tofu, and hard-boiled eggs to the pot. Continue to simmer for another 10 minutes, allowing the flavors to infuse into the ingredients.
5. Taste the broth and adjust seasoning if necessary, adding more soy sauce or sugar according to your preference.
6. Once all the ingredients are heated through and tender, remove the kombu from the pot and discard.

7. Serve the Oden hot in bowls, along with some of the broth. You can serve Japanese mustard (karashi) on the side for dipping if desired.

Oden is a versatile dish, and you can customize it with your favorite ingredients. It's a wonderful dish to enjoy during the colder months, warming you up from the inside out with its comforting flavors. Enjoy!

Chirashi sushi (scattered sushi)

Ingredients:

For the sushi rice:

- 2 cups sushi rice
- 2 1/2 cups water
- 1/4 cup rice vinegar
- 2 tablespoons sugar
- 1 teaspoon salt

For the toppings:

- Assorted sliced raw fish (sashimi), such as salmon, tuna, yellowtail, or shrimp
- Assorted seafood, such as cooked shrimp, crabmeat, or scallops
- Vegetables, thinly sliced or julienned (e.g., cucumber, avocado, radish, carrot)
- Tamagoyaki (Japanese rolled omelette), sliced into strips
- Seaweed salad
- Pickled ginger (gari)
- Wasabi
- Soy sauce

Instructions:

1. Rinse the sushi rice under cold water until the water runs clear. Drain well.
2. In a rice cooker or pot, combine the rinsed rice and water. Cook the rice according to the manufacturer's instructions or until it's cooked and slightly sticky.
3. While the rice is cooking, prepare the sushi vinegar. In a small saucepan, combine the rice vinegar, sugar, and salt. Heat over low heat until the sugar and salt are dissolved. Remove from heat and let it cool.
4. Once the rice is cooked, transfer it to a large bowl and gently fold in the sushi vinegar using a rice paddle or spatula. Be careful not to smash the rice grains. Allow the rice to cool to room temperature.

5. While the rice is cooling, prepare the toppings. Slice the raw fish into thin pieces, prepare the seafood, and slice the vegetables and tamagoyaki.
6. Once the rice has cooled, assemble the chirashi sushi. Spread the sushi rice evenly in a large serving bowl or individual bowls.
7. Arrange the sliced raw fish, seafood, vegetables, tamagoyaki, seaweed salad, and pickled ginger on top of the sushi rice in an attractive pattern.
8. Serve the chirashi sushi with wasabi and soy sauce on the side.

Chirashi sushi is a beautiful and delicious dish that's perfect for showcasing the freshness and variety of ingredients. It's customizable based on your preferences and what's in season, making it a versatile and enjoyable meal for any occasion. Enjoy!

Oyakodon (chicken and egg rice bowl)

Ingredients:

- 2 boneless, skinless chicken thighs, thinly sliced
- 1 onion, thinly sliced
- 3 eggs
- 2 tablespoons soy sauce
- 2 tablespoons mirin (Japanese sweet rice wine)
- 1 tablespoon sugar
- 1 cup dashi (Japanese soup stock)
- 2 cups cooked Japanese short-grain rice
- Sliced green onions for garnish (optional)
- Nori (dried seaweed), thinly sliced for garnish (optional)

Instructions:

1. In a small bowl, whisk together the soy sauce, mirin, sugar, and dashi to make the sauce for oyakodon. Set aside.
2. Heat a large skillet or frying pan over medium heat. Add the thinly sliced onion and cook until softened, about 3-4 minutes.
3. Add the thinly sliced chicken thighs to the skillet and cook until they are no longer pink, about 3-4 minutes.
4. Pour the sauce mixture over the chicken and onions in the skillet. Bring the mixture to a simmer.
5. In a separate bowl, lightly beat the eggs. Slowly pour the beaten eggs over the chicken and onions in the skillet, distributing them evenly.
6. Cover the skillet and let the eggs cook until they are softly set, about 2-3 minutes. Be careful not to overcook the eggs; they should be slightly runny.
7. Once the eggs are cooked to your liking, remove the skillet from the heat.
8. To serve, place a serving of cooked rice in each bowl. Spoon the chicken, onions, and eggs over the rice, making sure to distribute the sauce evenly.
9. Garnish with sliced green onions and nori strips if desired.

Oyakodon is a comforting and satisfying meal that's easy to make at home. It's perfect for a quick weeknight dinner or a cozy weekend lunch. Enjoy!

Nabemono (Japanese one-pot dishes)

Ingredients:

- 300g thinly sliced beef (sirloin or ribeye)
- 1/2 block of firm tofu, cut into cubes
- 1 bunch of shungiku (edible chrysanthemum leaves) or spinach, cut into bite-sized pieces
- 1/2 napa cabbage, sliced
- 4 shiitake mushrooms, sliced
- 4-6 shimeji mushrooms, separated into clusters
- 1 onion, thinly sliced
- 1 leek, sliced diagonally
- 4-6 shirataki noodles (optional)
- 2 tablespoons vegetable oil
- 1/3 cup soy sauce
- 1/3 cup mirin (Japanese sweet rice wine)
- 1/4 cup sugar
- 1 cup dashi (Japanese soup stock)
- 4 eggs, beaten (for dipping)

Instructions:

1. In a large skillet or shallow pot, heat the vegetable oil over medium heat. Add the sliced onion and cook until softened.
2. Add the thinly sliced beef to the skillet and cook until it starts to brown.
3. Add the soy sauce, mirin, sugar, and dashi to the skillet. Stir well to combine and bring the mixture to a simmer.
4. Add the tofu, shungiku or spinach, napa cabbage, shiitake mushrooms, shimeji mushrooms, and shirataki noodles (if using) to the skillet. Arrange the ingredients evenly in the skillet.
5. Cover the skillet and let the ingredients simmer in the broth for about 5-7 minutes, or until the vegetables are tender and the beef is cooked through.
6. Once everything is cooked, remove the lid and let everyone at the table serve themselves directly from the skillet.
7. To eat Sukiyaki, dip the cooked ingredients into the beaten raw egg before enjoying.

Sukiyaki is typically served with steamed rice on the side, but you can also enjoy it on its own or with noodles if preferred. It's a hearty and comforting meal perfect for sharing with family and friends. Enjoy your homemade Sukiyaki!

Yakiniku (Japanese grilled meat)

Ingredients:

- 500g thinly sliced beef (such as ribeye or sirloin)
- 500g thinly sliced pork (such as pork belly or shoulder)
- Assorted vegetables, thinly sliced or cut into bite-sized pieces (such as bell peppers, mushrooms, onions, zucchini)
- Yakiniku sauce (can be store-bought or homemade, see below for recipe)
- Optional: salt and pepper for seasoning

For the yakiniku sauce:

- 1/2 cup soy sauce
- 1/4 cup mirin (Japanese sweet rice wine)
- 2 tablespoons sugar
- 2 cloves garlic, minced
- 1 tablespoon sesame oil
- 1 tablespoon sesame seeds (optional)

Instructions:

1. If making the yakiniku sauce from scratch, combine the soy sauce, mirin, sugar, minced garlic, sesame oil, and sesame seeds in a small saucepan. Heat over low heat, stirring occasionally, until the sugar is dissolved and the sauce is slightly thickened. Remove from heat and let it cool.
2. Preheat your grill (charcoal or gas) or tabletop grill to medium-high heat.
3. Season the thinly sliced beef and pork with salt and pepper if desired.
4. Thread the meat slices onto skewers or place them directly on the grill.
5. Grill the meat for 1-2 minutes on each side, or until cooked to your desired level of doneness.
6. While the meat is grilling, you can also grill the assorted vegetables until they are tender and lightly charred.
7. Once the meat and vegetables are cooked, serve them hot off the grill with the yakiniku sauce for dipping.
8. To eat yakiniku, dip the grilled meat and vegetables into the yakiniku sauce before enjoying.

Yakiniku is often served with steamed rice, lettuce leaves (for wrapping), and additional condiments such as kimchi or pickled vegetables. It's a delicious and sociable meal that's perfect for gatherings and special occasions. Enjoy your homemade yakiniku!

Omurice (Japanese omelette rice)

Ingredients:

For the fried rice:

- 2 cups cooked Japanese short-grain rice (preferably leftover and chilled)
- 100g chicken thigh or breast, diced
- 1/2 onion, finely chopped
- 1 small carrot, finely diced
- 1/2 cup frozen peas
- 2 tablespoons vegetable oil
- 2 tablespoons ketchup
- Salt and pepper to taste

For the omelette:

- 4 large eggs
- 2 tablespoons milk or water
- Salt and pepper to taste
- 1 tablespoon butter

For garnish (optional):

- Ketchup
- Chopped parsley or green onions

Instructions:

1. Heat 1 tablespoon of vegetable oil in a large skillet or frying pan over medium heat. Add the diced chicken and cook until it's no longer pink. Remove the chicken from the skillet and set it aside.
2. In the same skillet, add another tablespoon of vegetable oil. Add the chopped onion and carrot, and cook until they are softened.
3. Add the frozen peas to the skillet and cook for a few minutes until they are heated through.

4. Return the cooked chicken to the skillet. Add the cooked rice and ketchup. Stir well to combine all the ingredients. Season with salt and pepper to taste. Cook for a few more minutes until everything is heated through.
5. Transfer the fried rice to a serving plate and shape it into a mound or any desired shape.
6. In a bowl, beat the eggs with milk or water. Season with salt and pepper to taste.
7. Heat the butter in the same skillet over medium-low heat. Pour the beaten eggs into the skillet and swirl to coat the bottom evenly.
8. Let the eggs cook until the bottom is set but the top is still slightly runny.
9. Carefully place the fried rice mound on one half of the omelette in the skillet.
10. Using a spatula, gently fold the other half of the omelette over the rice to encase it completely.
11. Slide the omurice onto a serving plate with the seam side down.
12. Drizzle some ketchup over the top of the omelette, and garnish with chopped parsley or green onions if desired.

Serve the Omurice hot and enjoy the delicious combination of fluffy omelette and flavorful fried rice!

Hiyashi chuka (cold ramen salad)

Ingredients:

For the noodles:

- 200g dried ramen noodles

For the toppings:

- 1 cucumber, julienned or thinly sliced
- 1 tomato, thinly sliced
- 2 eggs, boiled and thinly sliced
- 1/2 cup cooked chicken, shredded (optional)
- 1/4 cup ham or roast pork, thinly sliced (optional)
- 2 tablespoons toasted sesame seeds (for garnish)

For the dressing:

- 3 tablespoons soy sauce
- 2 tablespoons rice vinegar
- 1 tablespoon sesame oil
- 1 tablespoon sugar
- 1 teaspoon grated ginger
- 1 teaspoon grated garlic
- 1 teaspoon chili paste or sriracha (optional, for heat)

Instructions:

1. Cook the ramen noodles according to the package instructions. Once cooked, drain and rinse the noodles under cold water to stop the cooking process and cool them down. Drain well and set aside.
2. Prepare the toppings by slicing the cucumber, tomato, and boiled eggs. If using cooked chicken or ham, shred or slice them thinly.
3. In a small bowl, whisk together the soy sauce, rice vinegar, sesame oil, sugar, grated ginger, grated garlic, and chili paste (if using) to make the dressing. Adjust the seasoning to taste.

4. To assemble the Hiyashi Chuka, divide the cold ramen noodles among serving bowls.
5. Arrange the sliced cucumber, tomato, boiled egg, cooked chicken or ham (if using), and any other desired toppings over the noodles.
6. Drizzle the dressing over the top of each bowl, or serve it on the side for diners to add according to their preference.
7. Sprinkle toasted sesame seeds over the assembled bowls for garnish.
8. Serve the Hiyashi Chuka immediately and enjoy the refreshing flavors!

Feel free to customize the toppings and dressing according to your taste preferences. Hiyashi Chuka is a versatile dish that can be adapted with various ingredients, making it a perfect choice for a light and satisfying meal on a hot day.

Soba noodles

Ingredients:

- 200g soba noodles
- Water for boiling
- Optional toppings: sliced green onions, shredded nori (dried seaweed), grated daikon radish, sliced cucumber, tempura flakes, sesame seeds, soy sauce, and mirin for dipping sauce

Instructions:

1. Bring a large pot of water to a boil over high heat.
2. Add the soba noodles to the boiling water and cook according to the package instructions, usually about 4-5 minutes for dried noodles. Stir occasionally to prevent sticking.
3. While the noodles are cooking, prepare a bowl of ice water. This will be used to shock the noodles after they are cooked to stop the cooking process and cool them down quickly.
4. Once the noodles are cooked to your desired doneness (they should be tender but still have a slight chew), immediately drain them and transfer them to the bowl of ice water. Let them sit for about 30 seconds to cool down.
5. Drain the noodles again and rinse them under cold running water to remove any excess starch and prevent them from sticking together.
6. To serve cold soba noodles, arrange them in individual serving bowls or on a large platter. Garnish with your choice of toppings such as sliced green onions, shredded nori, grated daikon radish, sliced cucumber, tempura flakes, and sesame seeds.
7. In a small bowl, mix together soy sauce and mirin to create a dipping sauce for the noodles. Serve the dipping sauce alongside the cold soba noodles for dipping.
8. Alternatively, you can also serve soba noodles hot by skipping the step of cooling them down in ice water and serving them immediately after draining and rinsing.

Soba noodles are versatile and can be enjoyed in various dishes such as cold soba salad, hot noodle soups like soba noodle soup (soba no suimono) or soba noodle soup with tempura (tempura soba), or stir-fried soba noodles (yaki soba). They're a delicious and nutritious option that's perfect for any meal!

Karaage (Japanese fried chicken)

Ingredients:

- 500g boneless, skinless chicken thighs or breast, cut into bite-sized pieces
- 3 tablespoons soy sauce
- 2 tablespoons sake (Japanese rice wine) or dry sherry
- 2 cloves garlic, minced
- 1 teaspoon grated ginger
- 1 tablespoon sesame oil
- 1 tablespoon sugar
- 1 cup potato starch or cornstarch
- Vegetable oil for frying
- Lemon wedges or Japanese mayonnaise for serving (optional)
- Shredded cabbage or lettuce for serving (optional)

Instructions:

1. In a large bowl, combine the soy sauce, sake, minced garlic, grated ginger, sesame oil, and sugar to make the marinade.
2. Add the bite-sized pieces of chicken to the marinade, making sure they are well coated. Cover the bowl and let the chicken marinate in the refrigerator for at least 30 minutes, or up to 4 hours for maximum flavor.
3. When ready to cook, remove the chicken from the marinade and discard any excess marinade.
4. Place the potato starch or cornstarch in a shallow dish or bowl. Dredge each piece of chicken in the starch, shaking off any excess.
5. Heat vegetable oil in a deep fryer or large skillet to 170-180°C (340-360°F).
6. Carefully add the coated chicken pieces to the hot oil in batches, being careful not to overcrowd the fryer or skillet. Fry the chicken for about 5-6 minutes, or until golden brown and crispy, turning occasionally to ensure even cooking.
7. Once the chicken is cooked through and crispy, remove it from the oil using a slotted spoon and transfer it to a plate lined with paper towels to drain excess oil.
8. Serve the Karaage hot, with lemon wedges or Japanese mayonnaise for dipping, and shredded cabbage or lettuce on the side for freshness.

Karaage is best enjoyed immediately while still hot and crispy. It's a delicious and satisfying dish that's sure to be a hit with family and friends!

Ankake yakisoba (stir-fried noodles with thick sauce)

Ingredients:

For the noodles and vegetables:

- 200g yakisoba noodles (or substitute with ramen noodles)
- 1 tablespoon vegetable oil
- 1/2 onion, sliced
- 1 carrot, julienned
- 1 bell pepper, sliced
- 1 cup cabbage, shredded
- 100g sliced pork belly or chicken breast (optional)
- 2 green onions, sliced (for garnish)
- Toasted sesame seeds (for garnish)

For the sauce:

- 1 tablespoon vegetable oil
- 2 cloves garlic, minced
- 1 teaspoon grated ginger
- 2 tablespoons soy sauce
- 2 tablespoons Worcestershire sauce
- 1 tablespoon oyster sauce
- 1 tablespoon sugar
- 1 cup chicken or vegetable broth
- 2 tablespoons cornstarch mixed with 3 tablespoons water (for thickening)

Instructions:

1. If using dried yakisoba noodles, cook them according to the package instructions until they are al dente. Drain and rinse them under cold water to stop the cooking process and prevent sticking. Set aside.
2. In a small bowl, mix together the soy sauce, Worcestershire sauce, oyster sauce, and sugar to make the sauce. Set aside.
3. Heat 1 tablespoon of vegetable oil in a large skillet or wok over medium-high heat. Add the sliced onion, carrot, bell pepper, cabbage, and sliced pork or

chicken (if using). Stir-fry for 3-4 minutes, or until the vegetables are tender and the meat is cooked through.
4. Add the cooked noodles to the skillet or wok with the vegetables and meat. Stir-fry everything together for another 2-3 minutes, or until the noodles are heated through.
5. In a separate small saucepan, heat 1 tablespoon of vegetable oil over medium heat. Add the minced garlic and grated ginger, and cook for 1-2 minutes until fragrant.
6. Pour the sauce mixture into the saucepan with the garlic and ginger. Stir well to combine.
7. Add the chicken or vegetable broth to the saucepan and bring the mixture to a simmer.
8. Gradually add the cornstarch slurry to the sauce, stirring constantly, until the sauce thickens to your desired consistency.
9. Pour the thickened sauce over the stir-fried noodles and vegetables in the skillet or wok. Toss everything together until the noodles and vegetables are evenly coated with the sauce.
10. Transfer the Ankake Yakisoba to serving plates or bowls. Garnish with sliced green onions and toasted sesame seeds.

Serve the Ankake Yakisoba hot and enjoy the delicious combination of savory noodles and vegetables with a thick, flavorful sauce!

Hambagu (Japanese hamburger steak)

Ingredients:

For the hamburger patties:

- 500g ground beef or a mixture of beef and pork
- 1 small onion, finely chopped
- 1/2 cup panko breadcrumbs
- 1 egg
- 1 tablespoon Worcestershire sauce
- 1 tablespoon soy sauce
- Salt and pepper to taste
- Vegetable oil for cooking

For the sauce:

- 1/2 cup beef or chicken broth
- 2 tablespoons soy sauce
- 2 tablespoons Worcestershire sauce
- 1 tablespoon ketchup
- 1 teaspoon sugar
- 1 teaspoon cornstarch mixed with 1 tablespoon water (optional, for thickening)

Instructions:

1. In a large mixing bowl, combine the ground beef, finely chopped onion, panko breadcrumbs, egg, Worcestershire sauce, soy sauce, salt, and pepper. Use your hands to mix everything together until well combined.
2. Divide the mixture into equal portions and shape each portion into a round patty, about 1-inch thick.
3. Heat a tablespoon of vegetable oil in a large skillet or frying pan over medium heat. Once the oil is hot, add the hamburger patties to the skillet.
4. Cook the patties for about 5-6 minutes on each side, or until they are browned and cooked through. You may need to cook them in batches depending on the size of your skillet.

5. While the patties are cooking, prepare the sauce. In a small saucepan, combine the beef or chicken broth, soy sauce, Worcestershire sauce, ketchup, and sugar. Bring the mixture to a simmer over medium heat.
6. If you prefer a thicker sauce, you can add the cornstarch slurry to the saucepan and stir until the sauce thickens slightly.
7. Once the hamburger patties are cooked through, transfer them to a serving plate.
8. Pour the sauce over the hamburger patties, coating them evenly.
9. Serve the Hambagu hot, with rice and steamed vegetables on the side if desired.

Enjoy your homemade Hambagu, a delicious and satisfying Japanese comfort food!

Tonjiru (pork miso soup)

Ingredients:

- 200g thinly sliced pork belly or shoulder
- 1/2 onion, thinly sliced
- 1 carrot, thinly sliced
- 1 potato, peeled and diced
- 1/2 cup daikon radish, peeled and diced
- 1/2 cup shiitake mushrooms, sliced
- 2 green onions, sliced
- 4 cups dashi (Japanese soup stock)
- 3 tablespoons miso paste (white or red miso)
- 1 tablespoon soy sauce
- 1 tablespoon mirin (Japanese sweet rice wine)
- 1 tablespoon vegetable oil
- Salt and pepper to taste
- Optional: tofu, konjac (konnyaku), or other vegetables of your choice

Instructions:

1. Heat the vegetable oil in a large pot over medium heat. Add the thinly sliced pork and cook until it's browned.
2. Add the sliced onion to the pot and cook until it's softened.
3. Add the diced carrot, potato, daikon radish, and shiitake mushrooms to the pot. Stir well to combine with the pork and onion.
4. Pour the dashi (Japanese soup stock) into the pot and bring it to a simmer. Let the vegetables cook until they're tender, about 10-15 minutes.
5. In a small bowl, mix the miso paste with a ladleful of the hot broth until it's smooth and dissolved. Add the miso mixture back into the pot.
6. Add the soy sauce and mirin to the pot. Stir well to combine. Season with salt and pepper to taste.
7. If using tofu, add it to the pot and let it heat through for a few minutes.
8. Just before serving, add the sliced green onions to the pot.
9. Ladle the Tonjiru into serving bowls and serve hot.

Tonjiru is a versatile dish, and you can customize it with your favorite ingredients. It's a comforting and nutritious soup that's perfect for warming up on chilly days. Enjoy your homemade Tonjiru!

Tamagoyaki (Japanese rolled omelette)

Ingredients:

- 4 large eggs
- 2 tablespoons dashi (Japanese soup stock) or water
- 2 tablespoons sugar
- 1 tablespoon soy sauce
- 1/2 teaspoon salt
- Vegetable oil for cooking

Instructions:

1. In a mixing bowl, crack the eggs and beat them well with a fork or whisk until they're smooth and uniform in color.
2. Add the dashi (or water), sugar, soy sauce, and salt to the beaten eggs. Mix well to combine and dissolve the sugar and salt.
3. Heat a tamagoyaki pan or a square frying pan over medium heat. Brush the pan lightly with vegetable oil.
4. Pour a thin layer of the egg mixture into the pan, just enough to cover the bottom. Tilt the pan to spread the egg evenly and create a thin layer.
5. Once the bottom of the egg is set but the top is still slightly runny, start rolling it up from one end of the pan using chopsticks or a spatula.
6. Push the rolled egg to the far end of the pan, leaving some space at the end.
7. Brush the empty space in the pan with more oil and pour another thin layer of the egg mixture over the rolled egg. Tilt the pan to spread the egg evenly, making sure it covers the rolled egg.
8. Once the new layer of egg is set but still slightly runny on top, roll it up again towards the far end of the pan, incorporating it into the existing roll.
9. Repeat the process of adding oil, pouring egg mixture, and rolling until you've used up all the egg mixture and formed a thick roll of Tamagoyaki.
10. Transfer the rolled Tamagoyaki to a bamboo sushi mat or a cutting board. Use the mat or board to shape the Tamagoyaki into a neat rectangular shape.
11. Let the Tamagoyaki cool slightly before slicing it into thick slices.
12. Serve the sliced Tamagoyaki warm or at room temperature as a side dish or part of a meal.

Tamagoyaki is delicious on its own or served with a drizzle of soy sauce or a sprinkle of furikake (Japanese seasoning). Enjoy your homemade Tamagoyaki!

Dorayaki (Japanese pancakes filled with sweet red bean paste)

Ingredients:

For the pancake batter:

- 2 large eggs
- 1/2 cup granulated sugar
- 1 tablespoon honey or maple syrup
- 1 teaspoon vanilla extract
- 1 cup all-purpose flour
- 1 teaspoon baking powder
- 2-3 tablespoons water (adjust consistency as needed)
- Vegetable oil for cooking

For the filling:

- 1 cup sweet red bean paste (anko)

Instructions:

1. In a mixing bowl, beat the eggs and sugar together until pale and fluffy.
2. Add the honey or maple syrup and vanilla extract to the egg mixture. Mix well to combine.
3. Sift the flour and baking powder into the bowl with the egg mixture. Gently fold the dry ingredients into the wet ingredients until just combined. Be careful not to overmix.
4. Gradually add water to the batter, a tablespoon at a time, until you achieve a smooth and pourable consistency. The batter should be thick but still pourable.
5. Heat a non-stick skillet or griddle over medium heat. Lightly grease the skillet with vegetable oil.
6. Pour about 1/4 cup of the pancake batter onto the skillet to form a small circle, making sure to leave some space between each pancake as they will spread slightly.
7. Cook the pancakes for about 1-2 minutes, or until bubbles form on the surface and the edges start to set.
8. Flip the pancakes with a spatula and cook for an additional 1-2 minutes on the other side, or until golden brown and cooked through.

9. Remove the cooked pancakes from the skillet and transfer them to a plate. Cover them with a clean kitchen towel to keep them warm and moist while you cook the remaining pancakes.
10. Once all the pancakes are cooked, let them cool slightly.
11. To assemble the Dorayaki, spread a spoonful of sweet red bean paste (anko) onto the bottom side of one pancake. Place another pancake on top to sandwich the filling.
12. Repeat the process with the remaining pancakes and red bean paste until you've used up all the ingredients.
13. Serve the Dorayaki warm or at room temperature. They can be enjoyed as a snack, dessert, or with a cup of green tea.

Enjoy your homemade Dorayaki, and savor the delightful combination of fluffy pancakes and sweet red bean paste filling!

Yakisoba (Japanese stir-fried noodles)

Ingredients:

- 200g yakisoba noodles (fresh or dried)
- 100g thinly sliced pork belly, chicken breast, or shrimp (optional)
- 1/2 onion, thinly sliced
- 1 carrot, julienned
- 1 bell pepper, thinly sliced
- 1 cup cabbage, shredded
- 2 green onions, sliced diagonally (for garnish)
- Toasted sesame seeds (for garnish)
- Vegetable oil for cooking

For the yakisoba sauce:

- 3 tablespoons soy sauce
- 2 tablespoons Worcestershire sauce
- 1 tablespoon oyster sauce
- 1 tablespoon ketchup
- 1 tablespoon sugar
- 1/2 teaspoon grated ginger
- 1 clove garlic, minced
- 1 tablespoon sake or dry sherry (optional)

Instructions:

1. If using dried yakisoba noodles, cook them according to the package instructions until they're al dente. Drain and rinse them under cold water to stop the cooking process and prevent sticking. Set aside.
2. In a small bowl, mix together all the ingredients for the yakisoba sauce: soy sauce, Worcestershire sauce, oyster sauce, ketchup, sugar, grated ginger, minced garlic, and sake (if using). Set aside.
3. Heat a tablespoon of vegetable oil in a large skillet or wok over medium-high heat. If using meat or seafood, add it to the skillet and cook until it's browned and cooked through. Remove the meat or seafood from the skillet and set it aside.

4. Add a little more oil to the skillet if needed. Add the sliced onion, julienned carrot, thinly sliced bell pepper, and shredded cabbage to the skillet. Stir-fry the vegetables until they're tender-crisp.
5. Add the cooked yakisoba noodles to the skillet, along with the cooked meat or seafood (if using).
6. Pour the yakisoba sauce over the noodles and vegetables in the skillet. Stir well to combine and coat everything evenly with the sauce.
7. Continue to stir-fry the yakisoba for a few more minutes, or until everything is heated through and well combined.
8. Transfer the yakisoba to serving plates or bowls. Garnish with sliced green onions and toasted sesame seeds.
9. Serve the yakisoba hot and enjoy!

Yakisoba is a versatile dish, and you can customize it with your favorite ingredients such as mushrooms, bean sprouts, or even kimchi. It's a flavorful and comforting meal that's sure to be a hit with family and friends!

Ochazuke (rice with tea poured over)

Ingredients:

- Cooked Japanese short-grain rice
- Hot green tea or dashi broth (you can use instant dashi granules dissolved in hot water)
- Toppings of your choice (see suggestions below)

Optional toppings:

- Grilled salmon or trout fillet, flaked
- Umeboshi (pickled plum), thinly sliced
- Nori (dried seaweed), cut into thin strips
- Wakame (dried seaweed), rehydrated
- Tsukemono (Japanese pickles), such as takuan or cucumbers
- Scallions, thinly sliced
- Toasted sesame seeds
- Wasabi
- Shredded nori seaweed
- Furikake (Japanese rice seasoning)

Instructions:

1. Place a serving of cooked rice in a bowl. The amount of rice can vary depending on your appetite, but a typical serving size is around 1 cup.
2. If using hot green tea, brew it using your preferred method. If using dashi broth, dissolve instant dashi granules in hot water according to the package instructions.
3. Pour the hot green tea or dashi broth over the rice in the bowl. Start with a small amount and adjust to your desired consistency. Some people prefer their Ochazuke to be soupy, while others prefer it to be more like a sauce.
4. Add your choice of toppings to the Ochazuke. You can use one or a combination of toppings, depending on your preference. Feel free to get creative and use whatever ingredients you have on hand.

5. Serve the Ochazuke immediately while it's still hot. Enjoy it as a light and comforting meal or snack.

Ochazuke is a versatile dish, and the toppings can be customized to suit your taste. It's a great way to enjoy the comforting combination of warm rice and flavorful broth, especially on a cold day or when you're in need of a quick and easy meal.

Chazuke (Japanese rice soup)

Ingredients:

- Cooked Japanese short-grain rice
- Hot green tea, dashi broth, or hot water
- Toppings of your choice (see suggestions below)

Optional toppings:

- Grilled salmon or trout fillet, flaked
- Umeboshi (pickled plum), thinly sliced
- Nori (dried seaweed), cut into thin strips
- Wakame (dried seaweed), rehydrated
- Tsukemono (Japanese pickles), such as takuan or cucumbers
- Scallions, thinly sliced
- Toasted sesame seeds
- Wasabi
- Shredded nori seaweed
- Furikake (Japanese rice seasoning)

Instructions:

1. Place a serving of cooked rice in a bowl. The amount of rice can vary depending on your appetite, but a typical serving size is around 1 cup.
2. If using hot green tea, brew it using your preferred method. If using dashi broth, dissolve instant dashi granules in hot water according to the package instructions. Alternatively, you can simply use hot water.
3. Pour the hot green tea, dashi broth, or hot water over the rice in the bowl. Start with a small amount and adjust to your desired consistency. Some people prefer their Chazuke to be soupy, while others prefer it to be more like a sauce.
4. Add your choice of toppings to the Chazuke. You can use one or a combination of toppings, depending on your preference. Feel free to get creative and use whatever ingredients you have on hand.
5. Serve the Chazuke immediately while it's still hot. Enjoy it as a light and comforting meal or snack.

Chazuke is a versatile dish, and the toppings can be customized to suit your taste. It's a great way to enjoy the comforting combination of warm rice and flavorful broth, especially on a cold day or when you're in need of a quick and easy meal.

Oshizushi (pressed sushi)

Ingredients:

- Sushi rice (cooked and seasoned with rice vinegar, sugar, and salt)
- Sushi toppings of your choice (such as cooked shrimp, smoked salmon, tuna, avocado, cucumber, pickled vegetables, etc.)
- Sushi mold (also called oshibako) - you can use a specialized sushi mold or improvise with a small rectangular or square container lined with plastic wrap

Instructions:

1. Prepare the sushi rice by cooking Japanese short-grain rice according to the package instructions. Once cooked, transfer the rice to a large bowl and season it with a mixture of rice vinegar, sugar, and salt. Gently mix the seasoning into the rice using a cutting motion to avoid crushing the grains. Let the seasoned rice cool to room temperature.
2. Prepare your choice of sushi toppings by slicing them into thin strips or small pieces that will fit into the sushi mold.
3. Line the bottom of the sushi mold with plastic wrap, ensuring that there is enough overhang to cover the top of the mold later.
4. Place a layer of sushi rice into the bottom of the mold, using a spoon or spatula to press it firmly and evenly into the bottom of the mold.
5. Add a layer of your sushi toppings on top of the rice, arranging them evenly across the surface.
6. Add another layer of sushi rice on top of the toppings, pressing it down firmly to compact the ingredients and fill any gaps.
7. Fold the plastic wrap over the top of the sushi mold to cover the rice completely. Press down firmly on the wrap to compress the sushi.
8. Carefully remove the sushi from the mold by lifting the plastic wrap. Slice the pressed sushi into individual pieces using a sharp knife, wiping the blade clean between cuts to ensure clean edges.
9. Serve the Oshizushi on a plate, garnished with additional toppings if desired. It can be enjoyed with soy sauce, wasabi, and pickled ginger on the side.

Oshizushi is a versatile dish, and you can customize it with your favorite sushi toppings. It's a fun and delicious way to enjoy sushi at home!

Tofu dishes (such as agedashi tofu or tofu steak)

Ingredients:

- 1 block of firm tofu, drained and cut into cubes
- Cornstarch for dusting
- Vegetable oil for frying
- Dashi broth:
    - 1 cup dashi (Japanese soup stock)
    - 1 tablespoon soy sauce
    - 1 tablespoon mirin (Japanese sweet rice wine)
    - 1 tablespoon sake (Japanese rice wine)
- Toppings:
    - Grated daikon radish
    - Thinly sliced green onions
    - Shredded nori (dried seaweed)
    - Bonito flakes (katsuobushi) (optional)

Instructions:

1. Pat the tofu dry with paper towels and cut it into cubes. Dust each tofu cube lightly with cornstarch.
2. Heat vegetable oil in a deep frying pan or pot over medium-high heat. Fry the tofu cubes until they're golden brown and crispy on all sides. Remove them from the oil and drain them on paper towels.
3. In a separate saucepan, combine the dashi, soy sauce, mirin, and sake. Bring the mixture to a simmer.
4. Place the fried tofu cubes in serving bowls and pour the hot dashi broth over them.
5. Garnish the Agedashi Tofu with grated daikon radish, sliced green onions, shredded nori, and bonito flakes (if using).
6. Serve the Agedashi Tofu immediately as an appetizer or part of a meal.
7. Tofu Steak:

Ingredients:

- 1 block of firm tofu, drained and cut into thick slices
- Marinade:
    - 3 tablespoons soy sauce
    - 2 tablespoons mirin (Japanese sweet rice wine)
    - 1 tablespoon sesame oil
    - 1 tablespoon grated ginger
    - 2 cloves garlic, minced
    - Salt and pepper to taste
- Vegetable oil for frying
- Toppings:
    - Sliced mushrooms (shiitake, button, or your choice)
    - Sliced onions
    - Chopped green onions
    - Sesame seeds for garnish

Instructions:

1. In a shallow dish, mix together the soy sauce, mirin, sesame oil, grated ginger, minced garlic, salt, and pepper to make the marinade.
2. Place the tofu slices in the marinade, ensuring they're evenly coated. Let them marinate for at least 30 minutes, or longer for more flavor.
3. Heat vegetable oil in a skillet or frying pan over medium-high heat. Remove the tofu slices from the marinade (reserve the marinade) and fry them until they're golden brown and crispy on both sides. Remove them from the pan and set them aside.
4. In the same pan, add the sliced mushrooms and onions. Cook them until they're softened and caramelized.
5. Pour the reserved marinade into the pan with the mushrooms and onions. Let it simmer until it thickens slightly into a sauce.
6. Place the fried tofu slices on serving plates and spoon the mushroom and onion sauce over them.
7. Garnish the Tofu Steak with chopped green onions and sesame seeds.
8. Serve the Tofu Steak hot, accompanied by steamed rice or your favorite side dishes.

These tofu dishes are delicious and packed with flavor, making them perfect for vegetarians and tofu lovers alike!

Kaiseki (traditional Japanese multi-course meal)

Sakizuke (Appetizer) - Seasonal Vegetable Tempura:

1. Ingredients:
- Assorted seasonal vegetables (e.g., sweet potato, eggplant, bell pepper)
- Tempura batter mix
- Vegetable oil for frying
- Tentsuyu dipping sauce (soy sauce, mirin, dashi)

Instructions:

1. Prepare the tentsuyu dipping sauce by combining soy sauce, mirin, and dashi in a saucepan. Heat gently until warmed through, then set aside.
2. Slice the seasonal vegetables into thin pieces.
3. Prepare the tempura batter according to the package instructions.
4. Heat vegetable oil in a deep fryer or large pot to 350°F (180°C).
5. Dip the vegetable slices into the tempura batter, shaking off any excess, and carefully lower them into the hot oil.
6. Fry the vegetables until golden brown and crispy, then remove them from the oil and drain on paper towels.
7. Serve the tempura immediately with the tentsuyu dipping sauce on the side.

Hassun (Assortment) - Sashimi Platter:

8. Ingredients:
- Assorted fresh sashimi-grade fish (e.g., tuna, salmon, yellowtail)
- Soy sauce, wasabi, pickled ginger for serving

Instructions:

1. Slice the fresh fish into thin pieces and arrange them on a serving platter.
2. Serve the sashimi with small bowls of soy sauce, wasabi, and thinly sliced pickled ginger on the side.

Mukozuke (Sashimi) - Sliced Sea Bream Sashimi:

3. Ingredients:
- Fresh sea bream fillet
- Soy sauce, wasabi, pickled ginger for serving

Instructions:

1. Slice the sea bream fillet into thin slices.
2. Arrange the slices on a serving plate.
3. Serve the sashimi with small bowls of soy sauce, wasabi, and thinly sliced pickled ginger on the side.

Takiawase (Simmered Dish) - Simmered Mushroom and Tofu:

4. Ingredients:
- Assorted mushrooms (e.g., shiitake, shimeji)
- Firm tofu
- Dashi stock (made from kombu and bonito flakes)
- Soy sauce, mirin, sake
- Green onions for garnish

Instructions:

1. Cut the tofu into cubes and slice the mushrooms.
2. In a saucepan, combine dashi stock, soy sauce, mirin, and sake. Bring to a simmer.
3. Add the tofu and mushrooms to the simmering broth and cook until heated through.
4. Serve the simmered tofu and mushrooms in small bowls, garnished with sliced green onions.

Yakimono (Grilled Dish) - Grilled Miso-Marinated Black Cod:

5. Ingredients:
- Black cod fillets
- Miso paste
- Soy sauce, mirin, sake

- Sugar
- Grated ginger

Instructions:

1. In a bowl, mix together miso paste, soy sauce, mirin, sake, sugar, and grated ginger to make the marinade.
2. Coat the black cod fillets with the marinade and let them marinate for at least 30 minutes.
3. Preheat a grill or broiler to medium-high heat.
4. Grill the black cod fillets until cooked through and caramelized on the outside.
5. Serve the grilled black cod fillets on a plate.

Su-zakana (Vinegared Dish) - Sunomono (Vinegared Cucumber Salad):

6. Ingredients:
- Cucumber
- Wakame seaweed
- Octopus or shrimp
- Rice vinegar, sugar, salt
- Sesame seeds for garnish

Instructions:

1. Slice the cucumber thinly and rehydrate the wakame seaweed.
2. Cook the octopus or shrimp until tender, then slice thinly.
3. In a bowl, mix together rice vinegar, sugar, and salt to make the dressing.
4. Combine the cucumber, wakame seaweed, and sliced octopus or shrimp in the dressing.
5. Chill the salad in the refrigerator until ready to serve.
6. Serve the vinegared cucumber salad in small bowls, garnished with sesame seeds.

Shiizakana (Hot Pot Dish) - Sukiyaki:

7. Ingredients:

- Thinly sliced beef
- Tofu
- Shirataki noodles
- Vegetables (e.g., napa cabbage, mushrooms, green onions)
- Sukiyaki sauce (made from soy sauce, mirin, sugar, sake)
- Raw egg for dipping

Instructions:

1. Prepare the sukiyaki sauce by combining soy sauce, mirin, sugar, and sake in a saucepan.
2. Heat a tabletop grill or hot pot over medium heat.
3. Add the thinly sliced beef, tofu, shirataki noodles, and vegetables to the hot pot.
4. Pour the sukiyaki sauce over the ingredients and simmer until cooked through.
5. Dip the cooked ingredients into raw beaten egg before eating.

Gohan (Rice) and Ko no Mono (Pickles):

6. Ingredients:
- Steamed white rice
- Assorted Japanese pickles (tsukemono)

Instructions:

1. Serve steamed white rice in small bowls.
2. Serve assorted Japanese pickles on the side.

Mizumono (Dessert) - Matcha Tiramisu:

3. Ingredients:
- Matcha powder
- Sponge cake
- Mascarpone cheese
- Sugar
- Whipped cream
- Dark chocolate shavings

Instructions:

1. Prepare matcha-flavored sponge cake according to package instructions.
2. In a bowl, mix together mascarpone cheese, sugar, and matcha powder to taste.
3. Layer the sponge cake with the matcha mascarpone mixture and whipped cream in serving glasses.
4. Chill the tiramisu in the refrigerator until ready to serve.
5. Garnish with dark chocolate shavings before serving.

This simplified kaiseki-inspired meal captures the essence of traditional Japanese cuisine while providing a manageable cooking experience at home. Feel free to adjust the recipes and ingredients based on your preferences and what's available locally. Enjoy your kaiseki-inspired culinary journey!

Matcha desserts (such as matcha ice cream or matcha cake)

1. Matcha Ice Cream:

Ingredients:

- 2 cups heavy cream
- 1 cup whole milk
- 3/4 cup granulated sugar
- 3 tablespoons matcha powder
- 1 teaspoon vanilla extract
- Pinch of salt

Instructions:

1. In a saucepan, combine the heavy cream, whole milk, and granulated sugar. Heat over medium heat, stirring occasionally, until the sugar has dissolved and the mixture is warm but not boiling.
2. Remove the saucepan from the heat and whisk in the matcha powder until smooth and fully incorporated.
3. Stir in the vanilla extract and a pinch of salt.
4. Transfer the mixture to a bowl and cover with plastic wrap, pressing it directly onto the surface of the mixture to prevent a skin from forming.
5. Chill the mixture in the refrigerator for at least 4 hours or overnight until thoroughly chilled.
6. Once chilled, pour the mixture into an ice cream maker and churn according to the manufacturer's instructions until it reaches a soft-serve consistency.
7. Transfer the churned ice cream to a freezer-safe container and freeze for an additional 2-3 hours or until firm.
8. Serve the matcha ice cream scooped into bowls or cones, and enjoy!
9. Matcha Cake:

Ingredients:

- 1 3/4 cups all-purpose flour
- 1 tablespoon matcha powder
- 1 teaspoon baking powder

- 1/2 teaspoon baking soda
- 1/4 teaspoon salt
- 1/2 cup unsalted butter, softened
- 1 cup granulated sugar
- 2 large eggs
- 1 teaspoon vanilla extract
- 3/4 cup buttermilk

Instructions:

1. Preheat your oven to 350°F (175°C). Grease and flour a 9-inch round cake pan or line it with parchment paper.
2. In a medium bowl, whisk together the all-purpose flour, matcha powder, baking powder, baking soda, and salt until well combined. Set aside.
3. In a large mixing bowl, cream together the softened butter and granulated sugar until light and fluffy.
4. Beat in the eggs, one at a time, until fully incorporated. Stir in the vanilla extract.
5. Gradually add the dry ingredients to the wet ingredients, alternating with the buttermilk, beginning and ending with the dry ingredients. Mix until just combined, being careful not to overmix.
6. Pour the batter into the prepared cake pan and spread it out evenly.
7. Bake in the preheated oven for 25-30 minutes, or until a toothpick inserted into the center comes out clean.
8. Remove the cake from the oven and allow it to cool in the pan for 10 minutes before transferring it to a wire rack to cool completely.
9. Once cooled, slice and serve the matcha cake. Optionally, dust the top with powdered sugar or drizzle with a matcha glaze for extra flavor.

These matcha desserts are sure to impress with their vibrant color and delightful flavor. Enjoy making and savoring these delicious treats!

Sake-steamed clams

Ingredients:

- 2 pounds fresh clams (such as littleneck or Manila clams), scrubbed clean
- 1/2 cup sake (Japanese rice wine)
- 2 cloves garlic, minced
- 1-inch piece of ginger, thinly sliced
- 2 green onions, thinly sliced
- Optional: red chili flakes or sliced fresh chili for heat
- Soy sauce for serving (optional)
- Fresh cilantro or parsley for garnish (optional)

Instructions:

1. Rinse the clams under cold water and scrub them clean to remove any sand or debris. Discard any clams with broken shells or that are open and do not close when tapped.
2. In a large pot or deep skillet with a lid, heat the sake over medium-high heat until it begins to simmer.
3. Add the minced garlic, sliced ginger, and optional chili flakes or fresh chili to the pot. Stir and let them cook for about 1 minute to release their flavors.
4. Add the cleaned clams to the pot and cover with the lid. Steam the clams for about 5-7 minutes, or until they have opened. Discard any clams that do not open after steaming.
5. Once the clams have opened, remove the pot from the heat and transfer the steamed clams to serving bowls using a slotted spoon.
6. Strain the cooking liquid through a fine mesh sieve to remove any grit or impurities. Pour the strained cooking liquid over the steamed clams in the serving bowls.
7. Garnish the sake-steamed clams with thinly sliced green onions and fresh cilantro or parsley, if desired.
8. Serve the sake-steamed clams immediately, with soy sauce on the side for dipping if desired.

Savor the tender and flavorful clams along with the fragrant broth infused with the essence of sake, garlic, and ginger. This dish pairs well with steamed rice and a side of crunchy pickled vegetables for a satisfying meal. Enjoy!

Horenso no goma-ae (spinach with sesame dressing)

Ingredients:

- 1 bunch of spinach
- 2 tablespoons toasted sesame seeds
- 1 tablespoon soy sauce
- 1 tablespoon sugar
- 1 tablespoon mirin (Japanese sweet rice wine)
- 1 teaspoon sesame oil

Instructions:

1. Start by washing the spinach thoroughly under cold water to remove any dirt or grit. Trim off any tough stems or roots.
2. Bring a pot of water to a boil and add a pinch of salt. Prepare a bowl of ice water on the side.
3. Blanch the spinach in the boiling water for about 30 seconds to 1 minute, or until the leaves are wilted but still vibrant green.
4. Immediately remove the spinach from the boiling water and transfer it to the bowl of ice water to stop the cooking process and preserve its color. Let it cool for a minute, then drain and squeeze out excess water from the spinach.
5. Toast the sesame seeds in a dry skillet over medium heat until they are golden brown and fragrant. Be careful not to burn them. Once toasted, transfer the sesame seeds to a mortar and pestle or a food processor and grind them into a coarse powder.
6. In a small bowl, combine the ground sesame seeds with soy sauce, sugar, mirin, and sesame oil. Mix well until the sugar is dissolved and the dressing is smooth.
7. Place the blanched spinach in a serving bowl and pour the sesame dressing over the spinach.
8. Toss the spinach gently in the dressing until it is evenly coated.
9. Serve the horenso no goma-ae immediately as a side dish or part of a traditional Japanese meal.

Enjoy the tender spinach coated in the rich and nutty sesame dressing. This dish is a delightful combination of flavors and textures that pairs perfectly with steamed rice and other Japanese dishes.

Sunomono (Japanese cucumber salad)

Ingredients:

- 2 Japanese cucumbers or 1 English cucumber
- 1/4 cup rice vinegar
- 2 tablespoons sugar
- 1/2 teaspoon salt
- 1 teaspoon soy sauce
- 1 teaspoon sesame oil
- Toasted sesame seeds for garnish
- Thinly sliced seaweed (optional, for garnish)

Instructions:

1. Wash the cucumbers thoroughly and thinly slice them using a knife or a mandoline slicer. If using Japanese cucumbers, you can leave the skin on. If using an English cucumber, you may peel it if desired.
2. In a small bowl, mix together the rice vinegar, sugar, salt, soy sauce, and sesame oil until the sugar and salt are dissolved.
3. Place the sliced cucumbers in a large bowl and pour the vinegar dressing over them. Toss well to coat the cucumbers evenly.
4. Cover the bowl with plastic wrap or a lid and refrigerate for at least 30 minutes to allow the flavors to meld together and the cucumbers to marinate.
5. Before serving, drain any excess liquid from the cucumbers.
6. Transfer the sunomono to serving plates or bowls and garnish with toasted sesame seeds and thinly sliced seaweed, if desired.
7. Serve the sunomono chilled as a refreshing side dish or appetizer.

Enjoy the crisp and tangy flavors of this classic Japanese cucumber salad! It's a perfect accompaniment to sushi, sashimi, or any Japanese meal.

Zaru soba (cold buckwheat noodles with dipping sauce)

Ingredients:

For the soba noodles:

- 8 ounces (about 225 grams) dried soba noodles (100% buckwheat or a combination of buckwheat and wheat)
- Ice water (for rinsing the noodles)

For the dipping sauce (tsuyu):

- 1 cup dashi stock (you can use homemade dashi or instant dashi granules dissolved in water)
- 1/4 cup soy sauce
- 1/4 cup mirin (Japanese sweet rice wine)
- 1 tablespoon sugar
- Optional toppings: thinly sliced green onions, grated daikon radish, wasabi, nori seaweed strips

Instructions:

1. Cook the soba noodles according to the package instructions. Bring a large pot of water to a boil and add the soba noodles. Cook them for about 5-7 minutes, or until they are tender but still have a firm texture (be careful not to overcook them). Stir occasionally to prevent sticking.
2. While the noodles are cooking, prepare a bowl of ice water. Once the noodles are done, immediately drain them and rinse them thoroughly under cold running water to remove excess starch and stop the cooking process.
3. Transfer the rinsed noodles to the bowl of ice water and swish them around to cool them down quickly. This step helps the noodles retain their texture and prevents them from sticking together.
4. Drain the noodles well and arrange them on a bamboo or wire mesh sieve (zaru) to allow any remaining water to drip off. You can also place them on a plate lined with a clean kitchen towel.

5. In a small saucepan, combine the dashi stock, soy sauce, mirin, and sugar. Bring the mixture to a simmer over medium heat, then remove it from the heat and let it cool to room temperature.
6. Once the dipping sauce (tsuyu) has cooled, transfer it to individual serving bowls.
7. To serve, divide the cold soba noodles among serving plates or bowls. Optionally, garnish with thinly sliced green onions, grated daikon radish, wasabi, or nori seaweed strips.
8. Dip the noodles into the tsuyu dipping sauce and enjoy them chilled. You can also add toppings to the dipping sauce bowl for extra flavor.

Zaru soba is typically served with a side of sliced cucumbers or a small bowl of grated ginger to cleanse the palate between bites. It's a simple and refreshing dish that's perfect for hot summer days or any time you're craving a light and satisfying meal.

Gomoku gohan (rice cooked with mixed vegetables)

Ingredients:

- 1 1/2 cups short-grain Japanese rice
- 2 cups water
- 1 tablespoon soy sauce
- 1 tablespoon mirin (Japanese sweet rice wine)
- 1 tablespoon sake (Japanese rice wine)
- 1 tablespoon vegetable oil
- 1 small carrot, diced
- 1 small onion, diced
- 1/2 cup frozen peas
- 1/2 cup sliced shiitake mushrooms (fresh or rehydrated dried mushrooms)
- 1/4 cup bamboo shoots, sliced (canned or fresh)
- 1/4 cup sliced cooked chicken, ham, or shrimp (optional)
- Salt and pepper to taste
- Thinly sliced green onions for garnish

Instructions:

1. Rinse the short-grain rice under cold water until the water runs clear. Drain well.
2. In a medium saucepan, heat the vegetable oil over medium heat. Add the diced carrot and onion, and sauté until they start to soften, about 3-4 minutes.
3. Add the sliced shiitake mushrooms and bamboo shoots to the saucepan, and continue to sauté for another 2-3 minutes.
4. Add the rinsed rice to the saucepan, and stir to coat the rice with the vegetables and oil.
5. Pour in the water, soy sauce, mirin, and sake. Stir well to combine.
6. Bring the mixture to a boil, then reduce the heat to low. Cover the saucepan with a tight-fitting lid, and simmer for about 15-20 minutes, or until the rice is cooked and all the liquid has been absorbed.
7. During the last few minutes of cooking, add the frozen peas and sliced cooked chicken, ham, or shrimp to the saucepan, if using. Stir gently to incorporate the ingredients.
8. Once the rice is cooked and the vegetables are tender, remove the saucepan from the heat and let it sit, covered, for another 5 minutes to steam.

9. Fluff the gomoku gohan with a fork to mix the vegetables evenly throughout the rice. Season with salt and pepper to taste.
10. Serve the gomoku gohan hot, garnished with thinly sliced green onions for extra flavor and color.

Gomoku gohan makes a delicious and satisfying one-pot meal on its own, or it can be served as a side dish alongside grilled or roasted meats, fish, or tofu. Feel free to customize the recipe by adding your favorite vegetables and protein sources to suit your taste preferences. Enjoy!

Anmitsu (Japanese dessert with agar jelly and fruits)

Ingredients:

For the agar jelly:

- 2 teaspoons agar agar powder (or 2 tablespoons agar agar flakes)
- 4 cups water
- 1/2 cup sugar

For serving:

- Assorted fruits (such as strawberries, kiwi, mandarin oranges, peaches, and pineapple), sliced or cut into bite-sized pieces
- Sweetened red bean paste (anko)
- Canned fruit cocktail, drained
- Mochi (optional)
- Shiratama dango (optional)
- Kuromitsu (Japanese brown sugar syrup), for drizzling
- Matcha powder or kinako (roasted soybean flour), for garnish (optional)
- Ice cream (such as matcha or vanilla), for serving (optional)

Instructions:

1. Prepare the agar jelly:
    - In a medium saucepan, combine the water and agar agar powder (or flakes) and stir to dissolve.
    - Bring the mixture to a boil over medium heat, stirring occasionally.
    - Once boiling, reduce the heat to low and simmer for about 5 minutes, stirring constantly.
    - Add the sugar to the saucepan and continue to simmer for another 2-3 minutes, or until the sugar is completely dissolved.
    - Remove the saucepan from the heat and let the agar jelly mixture cool slightly.
2. Pour the agar jelly mixture into a shallow dish or square pan. Let it cool to room temperature, then refrigerate until set, about 1-2 hours.

3. Once the agar jelly is set, cut it into small cubes using a sharp knife.
4. Assemble the anmitsu:
    - Divide the agar jelly cubes among serving bowls or glasses.
    - Arrange the assorted fruits, sweetened red bean paste, canned fruit cocktail, mochi, and shiratama dango on top of the agar jelly cubes.
    - Drizzle kuromitsu (Japanese brown sugar syrup) over the fruits and jelly.
    - Optionally, sprinkle matcha powder or kinako (roasted soybean flour) over the anmitsu for added flavor and garnish.
    - Serve the anmitsu immediately, optionally accompanied by a scoop of ice cream on the side.
5. Enjoy the sweet and refreshing flavors of anmitsu as a delightful Japanese dessert!

Anmitsu is a versatile dessert, and you can customize it with your favorite fruits and toppings. It's perfect for serving at special occasions or as a refreshing treat on a hot day.

Katsudon (breaded and fried pork cutlet rice bowl)

Ingredients:

For the tonkatsu (breaded pork cutlet):

- 4 pork loin or pork tenderloin cutlets, about 1/2 inch thick
- Salt and pepper
- All-purpose flour, for dredging
- 2 eggs, beaten
- Panko breadcrumbs, for coating
- Vegetable oil, for frying

For the katsudon:

- Cooked Japanese rice
- 1 onion, thinly sliced
- 4 large eggs
- 2 cups dashi stock (or chicken broth)
- 4 tablespoons soy sauce
- 2 tablespoons mirin (Japanese sweet rice wine)
- 2 tablespoons sugar
- Thinly sliced green onions, for garnish
- Pickled ginger (beni shoga), for serving (optional)

Instructions:

1. Prepare the tonkatsu:
    - Season the pork cutlets with salt and pepper on both sides.
    - Set up a breading station with three shallow bowls: one with all-purpose flour, one with beaten eggs, and one with panko breadcrumbs.
    - Dredge each pork cutlet in the flour, shaking off any excess. Dip it into the beaten eggs, allowing any excess to drip off. Coat it evenly with panko breadcrumbs, pressing gently to adhere.
    - Heat vegetable oil in a large skillet or frying pan over medium heat. Fry the breaded pork cutlets for about 3-4 minutes on each side, or until golden brown and cooked through. Transfer them to a plate lined with paper towels to drain excess oil. Set aside.

2. Make the katsudon sauce:
    - In a separate saucepan, combine the dashi stock (or chicken broth), soy sauce, mirin, and sugar. Bring the mixture to a simmer over medium heat, stirring occasionally. Let it simmer for a few minutes until the sugar is dissolved and the flavors meld together. Remove from heat and set aside.
3. Assemble the katsudon:
    - In the same skillet or frying pan used to fry the pork cutlets, add the thinly sliced onions. Cook them over medium heat until they become soft and translucent.
    - Pour the prepared katsudon sauce over the onions in the skillet.
    - Slice each cooked tonkatsu into strips and arrange them on top of the onions in the skillet.
    - In a bowl, beat the eggs and pour them evenly over the tonkatsu and onions in the skillet.
    - Cover the skillet with a lid and let the eggs cook for a few minutes until they are set to your desired doneness.
4. Serve the katsudon:
    - Divide the cooked Japanese rice among serving bowls.
    - Using a spatula, carefully transfer the tonkatsu, onions, and egg from the skillet onto the rice in each bowl.
    - Garnish with thinly sliced green onions.
    - Serve the katsudon hot, optionally accompanied by pickled ginger on the side.

Enjoy the delicious combination of crispy tonkatsu, savory sauce, and fluffy rice in this comforting Japanese rice bowl dish!

Mochi (Japanese rice cakes)

Ingredients:

- 2 cups glutinous rice flour (also called sweet rice flour)
- 1 1/4 cups water
- Cornstarch or potato starch, for dusting (optional)

Instructions:

1. In a microwave-safe bowl, combine the glutinous rice flour and water. Stir well until the mixture is smooth and there are no lumps.
2. Cover the bowl loosely with plastic wrap or a microwave-safe lid, leaving a small vent for steam to escape.
3. Microwave the mixture on high for 2-3 minutes, depending on the wattage of your microwave. Stop and stir the mixture every minute to ensure even cooking.
4. The mochi is ready when it becomes translucent and sticky, with a thick, stretchy consistency.
5. Once cooked, immediately transfer the mochi to a clean surface dusted with cornstarch or potato starch to prevent sticking.
6. Let the mochi cool slightly until it's safe to handle, then knead it gently until it becomes smooth and elastic.
7. Divide the mochi into small portions and shape them into balls, squares, or discs, depending on your preference.
8. Your homemade mochi is now ready to be enjoyed! You can eat it plain, fill it with sweet red bean paste (anko), wrap it around pieces of fresh fruit, or use it as a topping for desserts.

Note: Mochi is best eaten fresh, as it tends to harden over time. If you have leftover mochi, store it in an airtight container at room temperature for up to 1-2 days, or freeze it for longer storage. To reheat frozen mochi, steam it for a few minutes until soft and pliable.

Enjoy the chewy texture and subtle sweetness of homemade mochi in your favorite desserts and snacks!

Oshiruko (sweet red bean soup)

Ingredients:

- 1 cup dried adzuki beans
- 6 cups water
- 1/2 cup granulated sugar (adjust to taste)
- Pinch of salt
- Mochi (glutinous rice cakes) or shiratama dango (sweet rice flour dumplings), for serving (optional)
- Toasted soybean flour (kinako) or roasted rice flour (katakuri-ko), for dusting (optional)
- Thinly sliced preserved cherry blossoms (optional, for garnish)

Instructions:

1. Rinse the dried adzuki beans under cold water to remove any dirt or debris. Drain well.
2. In a large pot, combine the rinsed adzuki beans and water. Bring the mixture to a boil over high heat, then reduce the heat to low and simmer, partially covered, for about 1 to 1 1/2 hours, or until the beans are soft and starting to break down. Stir occasionally and skim off any foam that rises to the surface.
3. Once the adzuki beans are cooked, mash them slightly with a spoon or potato masher to thicken the soup. Add more water if needed to achieve your desired consistency.
4. Stir in the granulated sugar and a pinch of salt, adjusting the sweetness to your taste preferences. Continue to simmer for another 10-15 minutes to allow the flavors to meld together.
5. Meanwhile, if using mochi or shiratama dango, prepare them according to the package instructions.
6. To serve, ladle the warm oshiruko into serving bowls. If using mochi or shiratama dango, place them in the bowls.
7. Optionally, dust the oshiruko with toasted soybean flour (kinako) or roasted rice flour (katakuri-ko) for added flavor and texture.
8. Garnish the oshiruko with thinly sliced preserved cherry blossoms for a traditional touch, if desired.
9. Serve the oshiruko immediately while warm, and enjoy the comforting sweetness of this classic Japanese dessert!

Oshiruko can be enjoyed as a dessert or snack on its own, or paired with a cup of green tea for a delightful treat. Adjust the sweetness and thickness of the soup to suit your preferences, and feel free to customize the toppings and garnishes according to what you have on hand.

Yudofu (hot tofu)

Ingredients:

- 1 block (about 14 ounces) silken tofu
- 4 cups dashi stock (Japanese soup stock)
- 2 tablespoons soy sauce
- 1 tablespoon mirin (Japanese sweet rice wine)
- 1 green onion, thinly sliced (for garnish)
- Grated ginger (optional, for serving)
- Ponzu sauce (optional, for serving)
- Shichimi togarashi (Japanese seven spice blend, optional, for serving)

Instructions:

1. Drain the silken tofu from its packaging and cut it into bite-sized cubes.
2. In a medium saucepan, combine the dashi stock, soy sauce, and mirin. Bring the mixture to a gentle simmer over medium heat.
3. Carefully add the tofu cubes to the simmering broth. Be gentle to avoid breaking the tofu.
4. Let the tofu simmer in the broth for about 5-7 minutes, or until heated through.
5. Once heated, remove the saucepan from the heat.
6. Ladle the yudofu into serving bowls, making sure to distribute the tofu cubes evenly.
7. Garnish each bowl of yudofu with thinly sliced green onions.
8. Optionally, serve grated ginger and ponzu sauce on the side for dipping or drizzling over the tofu.
9. You can also sprinkle shichimi togarashi (Japanese seven spice blend) over the yudofu for added flavor and spice.
10. Serve the yudofu hot as a comforting and nourishing dish.

Yudofu is often enjoyed as a light meal on its own or as part of a traditional Japanese meal. It's simple yet flavorful, allowing the delicate taste of the tofu to shine through. Feel free to customize the broth with additional ingredients such as kombu (dried kelp) or dried shiitake mushrooms for extra depth of flavor. Enjoy the warmth and comfort of homemade yudofu!

Gyunabe (beef hot pot)

Ingredients:

- 1 pound thinly sliced beef (such as ribeye or sirloin)
- 4 cups dashi stock (Japanese soup stock)
- 1/4 cup soy sauce
- 2 tablespoons mirin (Japanese sweet rice wine)
- 1 tablespoon sake (Japanese rice wine)
- 1 tablespoon sugar
- 1 onion, thinly sliced
- 1 carrot, thinly sliced
- 1/2 napa cabbage, chopped
- 4-6 shiitake mushrooms, sliced
- 1 block tofu, cut into cubes
- 2 green onions, thinly sliced (for garnish)
- Shichimi togarashi (Japanese seven spice blend, optional, for serving)
- Cooked Japanese rice, for serving

Instructions:

1. In a large pot or a nabe (Japanese hot pot), combine the dashi stock, soy sauce, mirin, sake, and sugar. Bring the mixture to a gentle simmer over medium heat.
2. Once the broth is simmering, add the thinly sliced beef to the pot. Allow the beef to cook briefly, just until it changes color and is no longer pink.
3. Add the sliced onion, carrot, and shiitake mushrooms to the pot. Let them simmer in the broth until they start to soften, about 5-7 minutes.
4. Add the chopped napa cabbage and tofu cubes to the pot. Continue to simmer until the vegetables are tender and the tofu is heated through.
5. Once all the ingredients are cooked, adjust the seasoning of the broth to taste, adding more soy sauce or mirin if desired.
6. To serve, ladle the gyunabe into individual serving bowls. Garnish each bowl with thinly sliced green onions and sprinkle with shichimi togarashi for extra flavor and spice.
7. Serve the gyunabe hot, accompanied by bowls of cooked Japanese rice for a complete meal.

8. Enjoy the warm and comforting flavors of homemade gyunabe with family and friends!

Gyunabe is a versatile dish, and you can customize it by adding your favorite vegetables and ingredients to the hot pot. Feel free to experiment with different combinations of meat, seafood, and vegetables to suit your taste preferences. Enjoy the cozy and communal experience of sharing gyunabe with loved ones around the dining table.

Hamachi kama (grilled yellowtail collar)

Ingredients:

- 2 yellowtail collars (hamachi kama)
- Salt, to taste
- Lemon wedges, for serving
- Soy sauce or ponzu sauce, for serving (optional)

Instructions:

1. Preheat your grill to medium-high heat. If you don't have a grill, you can use a broiler or a grill pan on the stovetop.
2. Pat the yellowtail collars dry with paper towels to remove any excess moisture.
3. Score the skin side of each collar with shallow cuts using a sharp knife. This helps the heat penetrate the collar evenly during grilling and prevents it from curling up.
4. Season both sides of the yellowtail collars generously with salt.
5. Place the collars on the preheated grill, skin side down. Grill for about 5-7 minutes on each side, or until the skin is crispy and golden brown, and the flesh is opaque and flakes easily with a fork. The exact grilling time will depend on the thickness of the collars.
6. Once the collars are cooked through and nicely grilled on both sides, remove them from the grill and transfer to a serving platter.
7. Serve the hamachi kama hot, garnished with lemon wedges for squeezing over the fish. You can also serve them with soy sauce or ponzu sauce on the side for dipping, if desired.
8. Enjoy the succulent and flavorful grilled yellowtail collar as a delicious appetizer or main course!

Hamachi kama is best enjoyed immediately while still hot off the grill. The combination of crispy skin and tender, juicy meat makes it a favorite dish in Japanese cuisine. Serve it alongside steamed rice and your favorite side dishes for a complete and satisfying meal.

www.ingramcontent.com/pod-product-compliance
Lightning Source LLC
LaVergne TN
LVHW081602060526
838201LV00054B/2040